D0604294

# CRIMINAL
## INVESTIGATIONS

## CRIME SCENE
## INVESTIGATION

# CRIMINAL INVESTIGATIONS

# CRIMINAL
## INVESTIGATIONS

## CRIME SCENE
## INVESTIGATION

## COLIN EVANS

CONSULTING EDITOR: **JOHN L. FRENCH**,

CRIME SCENE SUPERVISOR,
BALTIMORE POLICE CRIME LABORATORY

CHELSEA HOUSE
PUBLISHERS

An imprint of Infobase Publishing

# CRIMINAL INVESTIGATIONS: Crime Scene Investigation

Chelsea House
An imprint of Infobase Publishing
132 West 31st Street
New York NY 10001

**Library of Congress Cataloging-in-Publication Data**
Evans, Colin, 1948-
Crime scene investigation / Colin Evans ; consulting editor, John L. French. — 1st ed.
p. cm. — (Criminal investigations)
Includes bibliographical references and index.
ISBN-13: 978-0-7910-9405-1 (alk. paper)
ISBN-10: 0-7910-9405-7 (alk. paper)
1. Crime scenes—Juvenile literature. 2. Criminal investigation—Juvenile literature. 3. Evidence, Criminal—Juvenile literature. I. French, John L. II. Title.
HV8073.E925 2009                    363.25′2—dc22
2008030911

Chelsea House books are available at special discounts when purchased in bulk quantities for businesses, associations, institutions, or sales promotions. Please call our Special Sales Department in New York at (212) 967-8800 or (800) 322-8755.

You can find Chelsea House on the World Wide Web at
http://www.chelseahouse.com

Text design by Erika K. Arroyo
Cover design by Ben Peterson

*Cover:* State policeman Steven Green dusts the counter of a gas station for fingerprints after a report that a car thief may have stopped there after he abandoned a police cruiser.

Printed in the United States of America

Bang EJB 10 9 8 7 6 5 4 3 2 1

This book is printed on acid-free paper.

All links and Web addresses were checked and verified to be correct at the time of publication. Because of the dynamic nature of the Web, some addresses and links may have changed since publication and may no longer be valid.

# Contents

# Foreword

In 2000 there were 15,000 murders in the United States. During that same year about a half million people were assaulted, 1.1 million cars were stolen, 400,000 robberies took place, and more than 2 million homes and businesses were broken into. All told, in the last year of the twentieth century, there were more than 11 million crimes committed in this country.*

In 2000 the population of the United States was approximately 280 million people. If each of the above crimes happened to a separate person, only 4 percent of the country would have been directly affected. Yet everyone is in some way affected by crime. Taxes pay patrolmen, detectives, and scientists to investigate it, lawyers and judges to prosecute it, and correctional officers to watch over those convicted of committing it. Crimes against businesses cause prices to rise as their owners pass on the cost of theft and security measures installed to prevent future losses. Tourism in cities, and the money it brings in, may rise and fall in part due to stories about crime in their streets. And every time someone is shot, stabbed, beaten, or assaulted, or when someone is jailed for having committed such a crime, not only they suffer but so may their friends, family, and loved ones. Crime affects everyone.

It is the job of the police to investigate crime with the purpose of putting the bad guys in jail and keeping them there, hoping thereby to punish past crimes and discourage new ones. To accomplish this a police officer has to be many things: dedicated, brave, smart, honest, and imaginative. Luck helps, but it's not required. And there's one more virtue that should be associated with law enforcement. A good police officer is patient.

Patience is a virtue in crime fighting because police officers and detectives know something that most criminals don't. It's not a secret, but most lawbreakers don't learn it until it is too late. Criminals who make money robbing people, breaking into houses, or stealing cars; who live by dealing drugs or committing murder; who spend their days on the wrong side of the law, or commit any other crimes, must remember this: a criminal has to get away with every crime he or she commits. However, to get criminals off the street and put them behind bars, the police only have to catch a criminal once.

The methods by which police catch criminals are varied. Some are as old as recorded history and others are so new that they have yet to be tested in court. One of the first stories in the Bible is of murder, when Cain killed his brother Abel (Genesis 4:1–16). With few suspects to consider and an omniscient detective, this was an easy crime to solve. However, much later in that same work, a young man named Daniel steps in when a woman is accused of an immoral act by two elders (Daniel 13:1–63). By using the standard police practice of separating the witnesses before questioning them, he is able to arrive at the truth of the matter.

From the time of the Bible to almost present day, police investigations did not progress much further than questioning witnesses and searching the crime scene for obvious clues as to a criminal's identity. It was not until the late 1800s that science began to be employed. In 1879 the French began to use physical measurements and later photography to identify repeat offenders. In the same year a Scottish missionary in Japan used a handprint found on a wall to exonerate a man accused of theft. In 1892 a bloody fingerprint led Argentine police to charge and convict a mother of killing her children, and by 1905 Scotland Yard had convicted several criminals thanks to this new science.

Progress continued. By the 1920s scientists were using blood analysis to determine if recovered stains were from the victim or suspect, and the new field of firearms examination helped link bullets to the guns that fired them.

Nowadays, things are even harder on criminals, when by leaving behind a speck of blood, dropping a sweat-stained hat, or even taking a sip from a can of soda, they can give the police everything they need to identify and arrest them.

In the first decade of the twenty-first century the main tools used by the police include

- questioning witnesses and suspects
- searching the crime scene for physical evidence
- employing informants and undercover agents
- investigating the whereabouts of previous offenders when a crime they've been known to commit has occurred
- using computer databases to match evidence found on one crime scene to that found on others or to previously arrested suspects
- sharing information with other law enforcement agencies via the Internet
- using modern communications to keep the public informed and enlist their aid in ongoing investigations

But just as they have many different tools with which to solve crime, so too do they have many different kinds of crime and criminals to investigate. There is murder, kidnapping, and bank robbery. There are financial crimes committed by con men who gain their victim's trust or computer experts who hack into computers. There are criminals who have formed themselves into gangs and those who are organized into national syndicates. And there are those who would kill as many people as possible, either for the thrill of taking a human life or in the horribly misguided belief that it will advance their cause.

The Criminal Investigations series looks at all of the above and more. Each book in the series takes one type of crime and gives the reader an overview of the history of the crime, the methods and motives behind it, the people who have committed it, and the means by which these people are caught and punished. In this series celebrity crimes will be discussed and exposed. Mysteries that have yet to be solved will be presented. Readers will discover the truth about murderers, serial killers, and bank robbers whose stories have become myths and legends. These books will explain how criminals can separate a person from his hard-earned cash, how they prey on the weak and helpless, what is being done to stop them, and what one can do to help prevent becoming a victim.

John L. French,
Crime Scene Supervisor,
Baltimore Police Crime Laboratory

* Federal Bureau of Investigation. "Uniform Crime Reports, Crime in the United States 2000." Available online. URL: http://www.fbi.gov/ucr/00cius.htm. Accessed January 11, 2008.

# Introduction

Crime takes place everywhere and a crime scene can take almost any form. It may be a sidewalk, a house or apartment, the run-off from a mountain stream, perhaps a burnt-out car, a plundered bank, a computer hard drive, or even something as vast as several square miles of ocean. Whatever the location, crime scenes share one unifying thread—if the criminal is to be brought to justice, then all the evidence within that location needs to be recovered and processed with the utmost accuracy. This is where forensic science comes in.

Until the late nineteenth century, crime solving was a haphazard affair. It relied mainly upon eyewitnesses and confessions. The surprising thing is that, for the most part, this bare-bones technique worked quite well. But the new century brought with it a new set of problems. Gang crime was on the rise, so too was the homicide rate, and as people became more affluent they had more items worth stealing. As a consequence, burglaries and robberies soared. No doubt about it, the future looked bleak. Fortunately, though, help was at hand. For this was also an era of immense changes in the scientific world, changes that would have a direct bearing on the way law enforcement professionals tackle crime.

One of the most significant breakthroughs came in 1901 when the Nobel Prize-winning Austrian biologist Karl Landsteiner discovered the ABO blood grouping system. That same year in Germany Paul Uhlenhuth devised the precipitin test that, for the first time, enabled scientists to differentiate between human and non-human blood. Significant as these advances undoubtedly were, they can only rank as the princes of crime detection. When it comes

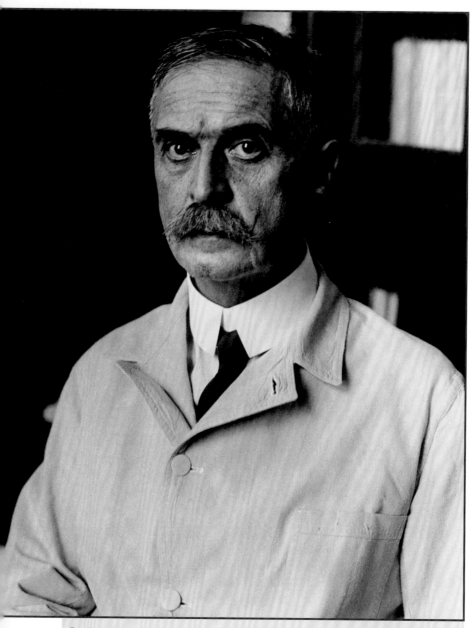

Doctor Karl Landsteiner discovered the ABO blood group in 1901, a significant breakthrough on the path to identifying criminals using crime scene evidence. *Bettmann/Corbis*

to crowning the undisputed king of the forensic science hill, there is only one real contender—the discovery in the late nineteenth century that no two human beings share the same fingerprint. This was a revolutionary breakthrough; at last, investigators had a definitive means of identification at their disposal. The hunt for fingerprints meant that, overnight, the crime scene took on a newfound importance.

One of the first to really grasp the significance of this change was a French forensic scientist named Edmond Locard. In 1910 Locard began work at the Laboratoire Intérregional de Police Technique in Lyons, where he evolved a theory that would change the course of criminology. The key to successful crime solving, he believed, lay in the proper and meticulous processing of the crime scene. At its heart was Locard's belief that whenever two human beings come into physical contact—no matter how briefly—something from one is transferred to the other. This has become known as Locard's Exchange Principle, and put in its simplest form it states: *Every contact leaves a trace.*

This is worth repeating: *Every contact leaves a trace.* And it applies wherever someone goes. If a person enters a room, that room is forever altered. That person might shed a skin cell or lose a single strand of hair. Perhaps a fiber from his or her clothes adheres to a table leg as he or she brushes past. A similar outcome might result when he or she sits down on a sofa. Conversely, when he or she exits the room, there is an almost 100 percent certainty that—somewhere on his or her person—lies a fragment of microscopic trace evidence that wasn't there when he or she entered. One thing is undeniable: the room is left in a different condition to how the person found it. Even outdoors, there is no escaping Locard's principle. The car driver who flees an accident may leave a flake of paint from his car or take a speck of grit on his tire or wheel arch as he or she makes a getaway. If investigators find that scrap of evidence, there's a good chance they've found the perpetrator.

Locard's Exchange Principle might sound deceptively simple, but for almost a century it has been *the* fundamental axiom of crime scene investigation. It drives everything. Fingerprints, trace evidence analysis, DNA profiling, chromatographic examination of unknown substances, in fact, just about every type of investigative technique covered in this book relies, in some measure, on Locard's Exchange Principle.

One hundred years on from Locard, forensic science is still pushing back the boundaries. When crime scene investigators are shown on those glossy TV dramas, it all looks so effortless. Moving ghostlike through the yellow-taped arena in their white Tyvek suits and face masks, they uncover the microscopic evidence invisible to everyone else, carry out brilliant analysis, explain how the crime was committed, and are usually able to point the finger at the guilty party. And all this happens in 44 minutes. If only it were that easy in real life.

Modern forensic science is time-intensive and, above all, painstaking. Ask any experienced crime scene investigator and he or she—and increasingly in recent years it is more likely to be a she—will tell you that their two overriding watchwords are *concentration* and *accuracy*. Walk into a fresh crime scene and that crime scene instantly becomes the most important of your career. One false step on your part could prove disastrous, maybe even allowing a dangerous criminal to escape justice. Keeping ahead of the game requires the utmost concentration. Accuracy is also vital. For without impeccable levels of precision—especially when it comes to the all-important chain-of-custody protocol discussed in Chapter 1—even the strongest case can fall flat on its face. Defense lawyers are always hungry for any hint of forensic sloppiness, no matter how slight. Give a skilled attorney just the slightest sniff of a slip-up and you can guarantee that it will soon get magnified into a blunder of Everest-like proportions, or so it may well be made to appear to the jury, because they've also seen the TV programs. They expect the forensic experts to deliver cast-iron opinions backed up by NASA-style levels of science. Indeed, so common has this expectation become among jurors that many in the judicial process now openly refer to this as "the CSI-effect."

An important point to remember is that a crime scene is never static. It changes every second that someone—even an investigator—is present. (There's that Locard Exchange Principle again.) This is why it's absolutely vital to make a visual record of the crime scene as soon as possible. As the renowned medical examiner Dr. Michael Baden puts it: "The first hour of a crime is critical."[1] Once a visual record has been made, it provides a permanent archive that

experts can refer to repeatedly for clarification. Videotape is used at most major crime scenes, and is useful for providing a general overview, but the still camera, with its ability to provide a sharply focused image that can be enlarged many hundreds of times if necessary, is unbeatable at recording the close-up detail of evidence. These photographs are absolutely crucial as they also allow more experts—for both the prosecution and the defense—to examine things as they were. In any general crime scene, the photographer will follow five steps. These are:

1. Secure the scene
2. Take preliminary notes
3. Take overview photographs
4. Make a basic sketch
5. Record each item of evidence

The basic principles of crime scene photography are little changed in 100 years. The only major difference is the number of photographs taken, typically 100–200 nowadays, compared to around 10 or so in times gone by. The equipment, however, has altered drastically.

The early photographer struggling with his bulky bellows camera ruled the roost until the introduction of the Graflex Speed Graphic, which became popular in the 1930s. (This is the hand-held "press" camera with a huge flash that we usually associate with crime movies about the gangster era.) Next came the 35mm SLR, which is still the camera of choice for many law enforcement agencies. In recent years there has been a shift to the digital camera. Not having to wait for an image to be developed may have speeded up the whole crime scene recording process, but digital photography has brought with it a whole new slew of problems. These chiefly concern the "alterability" of computer-generated images. (This criticism ignores the fact that 35mm film is equally capable of being altered, as a quick glance at any of the heavily airbrushed fashion magazines from 20 years ago will confirm.)

Once the evidence has been gathered, handled properly with a clear chain-of-custody protocol, and analyzed in accordance with sound scientific principles, it then needs to be tested in court. It is the duty of the forensic expert to present that evidence, but before this can happen, the court must decide on the admissibility of such evidence. This can be a very contentious area and is usually settled in accordance with what is called the Daubert Standard—established during the case *Daubert v. Merrell Dow Pharmaceuticals, Inc., 509 U.S. 579 (1993)*—in which the U.S. Supreme Court decided that federal judges are the gatekeepers of what is both "relevant" and "reliable" when it comes to scientific testimony.

If the evidence submitted for consideration passes the Daubert Standard, the expert witnesses get to present their findings to a judge and jury. This is the critical moment in the professional life of any crime scene investigator. They are expected to report the evidence as they found it—not to pass judgement on the guilt or innocence of the defendant—and to provide the jury with a reasonable interpretation of that evidence. Then comes the really hard part: having to support these conclusions in the face of an often withering cross-examination.

This can be problematic. Not all forensic experts make "expert" witnesses. Some are very fluent on the stand, expressing their findings in simple phrases that anyone can understand. Others mumble and quake under pressure. No prizes for guessing which witness most lawyers would prefer to have on board. Like it or not, in an adversarial system of justice, such as that employed in the United States of America, a trial is largely a contest of sales skills. Each side presents its case and the jury then decides which made the more compelling argument. For this reason the fluent expert witness is much in demand while others, no less talented as scientists, may fall by the wayside.

When forensic science was in its infancy at the beginning of the twentieth century, the typical expert witness was a far more dogmatic character than is generally the case in the modern courtroom. Opinions were expressed with an air of absolute certainty that brooked no argument. Sad to say this attitude is not entirely extinct. Also, in recent years, several discredited experts have been caught shading the evidence, either in favor of the prosecution or else to boost his or her ego and career. Unless there is a seismic shift in human nature this bias is unlikely ever to be completely eradicated, but that shouldn't prevent us from trying to root out these so-called experts. What is needed in court is the best science available, and that means doing the job right.

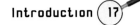

The battle against crime is nonstop. Consider the following: data published by the FBI for 2004 show that every 32 minutes someone is murdered in the United States; violent crimes occur at 23-second intervals; and each hour, 97 people are the victims of aggravated assault.[2] With these kinds of numbers the need for top quality crime investigators has never been higher.

# Fingerprints:
## Thomas Jennings, 1910

On the morning of February 4, 1906, a stockily built man hurried down the gangway of the S.S. *Carmania* just after it moored at New York harbor. Detective Sergeant Joseph A. Faurot of the New York Police Department (NYPD) was bursting with excitement. Later that day he summoned a press conference to share details of his trip to London. He enthused about how detectives from Scotland Yard had solved a recent double murder through a radical new crime-fighting technique: fingerprinting. Faurot told the fast-scribbling reporters how most European law enforcement agencies had already embraced the idea that no two people share the same fingerprint, and he asserted that it was high time American police did the same. A couple of months later Faurot got his big chance. A man calling himself Henry Johnson was arrested at the Waldorf-Astoria hotel on a charge of stealing jewelry from some fellow guests. Faurot listened skeptically to Johnson's story, delivered in a plummy English accent, and decided to wire his fingerprints to Scotland Yard to see if they had him on record. Faurot's suspicions were confirmed two weeks later: Johnson was a convicted thief, Daniel Nolan, who regularly used the alias Henry Johnson. Nolan was imprisoned, earning for himself the dubious distinction of being the first criminal in the United States caught through the use of fingerprints.

Now, Faurot thought, it was only a matter of time before finger-print testimony would figure prominently in a homicide case. He was right, but to Faurot's dismay, the NYPD commissioner didn't share his enthusiasm for the newfangled technique. History wasn't made on the streets of Manhattan, but half a continent away, in America's heartland.

Clarence Hiller lived with his wife and four children in a two-story house on West 104th Street, Chicago. Shortly after 2 a.m. on September 19, 1910, Mrs. Hiller was disturbed by a noise and noticed that a gaslight at the top of the stairs was out. She woke her husband and he hurried in his nightclothes to investigate.

At the top of the stairway Hiller encountered a stranger. The two men began to grapple. In the ensuing struggle both tumbled down the staircase. Moments later Mrs. Hiller heard two shots, then her husband's faint call for help. This was followed by the slamming of the front door. At the foot of the stairs, Mrs. Hiller found the lifeless body of her husband.

A neighbor, John C. Pickens, attracted by the shooting and the woman's screams, came on the double. By chance his son, Oliver, had met a policeman, Floyd Beardsley, just a short distance away. Both had heard the shots and arrived in seconds.

Beardsley quickly took stock of the situation. He learned how the killer, holding a lighted match at waist level so that his face remained in shadow, had first entered the bedroom of daughter, Clarice Hiller, age 15. From there he had creaked his way noisily into the bedroom of her 13-year-old sister, Florence. Jolted awake, Florence, thinking that the intruder might be her little brother, had cried out, "Is that you Gerald?" It was this cry that had disturbed Mrs. Hiller. The next thing Florence heard was her father on the landing. Just moments later the fatal struggle began.

An examination of the crime scene revealed some particles of sand and gravel near the foot of Florence's bed. There were also three unused cartridges found near the body. A more thorough search would have to wait until daylight. Even before it began, however, the killer had already been in custody for several hours, arrested on wholly unrelated charges.

At 2:38 a.m. on Vincennes Road, less than a mile east of the Hiller house, four off-duty officers were waiting for a streetcar when they noticed a man darting through the darkness, glancing furtively behind him. When challenged and told to empty his pockets, the stranger, who was sweating profusely, handed over a loaded .38 revolver. He gave his name as Thomas Jennings. There were fresh bloodstains on his clothing and he had injured his left arm; both the result, he said, of having fallen from a streetcar earlier that night.

Dissatisfied by Jennings's story, the officers took him to the station, which, by now, was buzzing with news of the Hiller murder. Immediately the wounded man became a prime suspect, especially when it was learned that just a few weeks earlier he had been freed from Joliet State Penitentiary after serving time for burglary.

A background check showed that on August 16, just two weeks after being released, under an assumed name and in violation of

## ♀ CHAIN-OF-CUSTODY PROTOCOL

All the scientific wizardry in the world is utterly worthless if the evidence has been improperly or illegally handled. Any hint of misconduct or negligence can ruin a case, raising the risk of that evidence being ruled inadmissible by the courts.

It is impossible to overstate the importance of crime scene integrity. This applies not just to how evidence is gathered, but what happens to that evidence afterward. Getting samples from the crime scene to the lab and then to the court in a satisfactory manner requires a valid paper trail or, more commonly nowadays, entry into a software program: the Laboratory Information Management System (LIMS). Whatever the method used, the outcome is called the chain of custody. It covers the seizure, custody, control, transfer, analysis, and disposition of all kinds of physical and electronic evidence. Each person—or link—in the chain must document his/her exposure to the material and what was done next with it. These details are recorded on a chain of custody card that provides a chronological description of who handled what and when. The procedure can best be demonstrated in the following example:

Police Officer A arrests a suspect and finds what appears to be drugs. Officer A places the suspicious substance in a bag, seals his parole, Jennings had purchased the .38 revolver. When examined, its cartridges were found to be identical to those lying next to Clarence Hiller's body. Jennings claimed not to have fired the gun since owning it, but the smell of fresh smoke and burned powder in two chambers of the cylinder said otherwise. This was later corroborated by a gunsmith. Two doctors who examined Jennings's injuries doubted they had occurred in a fall from a streetcar. They also found sand in his shoes very similar to that found at the crime scene.

The most significant discovery, however, occurred the next morning at the murder scene. Outside the rear kitchen window, through which the killer had entered, was a verandah surrounded by some railings. By chance, Clarence Hiller had painted these

and signs the bag, and enters it into evidence. The sealed bag is then transported by Officer B to the laboratory. At the lab a technician opens the bag, tests its contents, records the results, then reseals the bag and signs it. This bag is then placed back into evidence.

Should the case proceed to trial, Officer A has documentary evidence to show that he found and bagged the suspected drugs, which he then sealed. Since the next person in the chain of custody—Officer B, who transported the suspected drugs to the laboratory—never opened the bag, his presence in court will, most likely, be unnecessary. Finally, the lab technician can testify as to what the tests revealed. Because every link in the chain has been properly documented, the risk of evidence-tampering accusations has been greatly reduced. This, in a very basic form, is how the chain-of-custody protocol works. Occasionally, though, things do go wrong. In the above case, say, for example, Officer A is coming to the end of what has been a long, exhausting day. He's tired and ready to go home. Through a momentary lapse of concentration, he neglects to sign the bagged sample. If Officer B fails to spot this, then the chain is broken, with potentially devastating results for the investigation.

very railings just hours before his death, and etched into the fresh paint were what looked like four fingerprints. A closer look with a magnifying glass confirmed that it was indeed the impression of a left hand. That morning, officers from Chicago's Police Department Bureau of Identification (PDBI) carefully removed these railings and took them away for a full examination.

While other jurisdictions still pinned their criminal identification faith on the old system of bertillonage, the Chicago PD was fully committed to fingerprints. Bertillonage, a complicated identification method named after its French inventor Alphonse Bertillon, was based on cataloging dozens of different bodily measurements and distinguishing marks. It was ultimately proven unreliable. In the Hiller case, technicians from the PDBI made photographic enlargements of the fingerprints from the railings, which were then submitted to four experts for comparison with Jennings's prints. All four declared them to be identical. But would the courts permit this testimony?

No one in America had ever been convicted of murder on the basis of fingerprint testimony and Jennings's defense team was in no mood for their client to set any precedents. They argued vehemently that such evidence should be excluded. But the court disagreed.

A quartet of specialists testified at the trial: Michael P. Evans, his son William M. Evans, Edward Foster, and Mary Holland, America's first female fingerprint expert. All swore that Jennings's hand, and his alone, had left the prints on the railings. Their testimony led to a guilty verdict and a death sentence on February 1, 1911. Immediately, defense lawyers filed an appeal on grounds that fingerprinting was unworthy of the term *scientific* and that Illinois laws did not recognize such evidence.

Across the nation all legal eyes were on the Illinois Supreme Court, awaiting its decision. It came on December 21, 1911. In a historic ruling the court first sanctioned the admissibility of fingerprint evidence, then upheld the right of experienced technicians to testify as experts. Jennings's conviction and sentence were affirmed, and he was hanged on February 16, 1912.

Crime scene experts rarely have it so easy as in *People v. Jennings* (1911). Generally they have to work much harder to find usable prints. This is because fingerprint impressions basically fall into three types: latent, visible, and plastic, and of these, the most

A student dusts for latent fingerprints during a class session conducted by Pennsylvania State Police in February 2003. *AP/Keith Srokocic*

frequently found are of the latent type, which are invisible to the eye. These are formed by sweat, either from the hands themselves or by unconscious contact between the fingers and the face or other parts of the body where the sebaceous glands are situated. If a criminal touches any surface he or she is likely to leave a latent print, invisible to the naked eye, but this is more pronounced on smooth surfaces such as glass or polished wood.

Latent prints can be "developed" by a variety of means. The most common method is to dust the print with a high-contrast powder—white or gray/black, depending on the background—then to either photograph the print or lift it physically from the surface by means of a rubber "lifter" or transparent tape. This can then be stored and recorded. When latent prints are found on multicolored surfaces, it is customary to use fluorescent dusting powder.

The visible print, resulting from fingers dipped in either blood, grease, dirt, or some other contaminant, is rarely found at the crime scene, and shares its scarcity with the plastic print, which is an impression made on a soft surface such as tar or soap.

Although the life of a latent print is variable and can be degraded by atmospheric conditions and humidity, if made on a hard protected surface and left untouched, it is virtually permanent. Latent prints have been developed from objects found in ancient Egyptian tombs.

Since the 1970s the range of techniques to develop latent prints has expanded enormously. Even porous surfaces that previously defied analysis, such as concrete, are now giving up their secrets. The most common way is to use the cyanoacrylate—or super glue—method. This works by heating the sample in a small chamber with a blob of super glue. The fumes given off adhere to biological material such as the oil in fingerprints. Under a laser this biological material fluoresces, producing a clear image of the print. If, by chance, the cyanoacrylate happens to be the same color as the sample, then a biological stain can be introduced that will attach itself to the cyanoacrylate and thereby produce discernible prints.

Another technique used to process difficult-to-analyze surfaces or very old prints is Vacuum Metal Deposition (VMD). Not only can VMD lift latent prints from plastics, it does so with higher quality and greater definition than that of other techniques. Although VMD

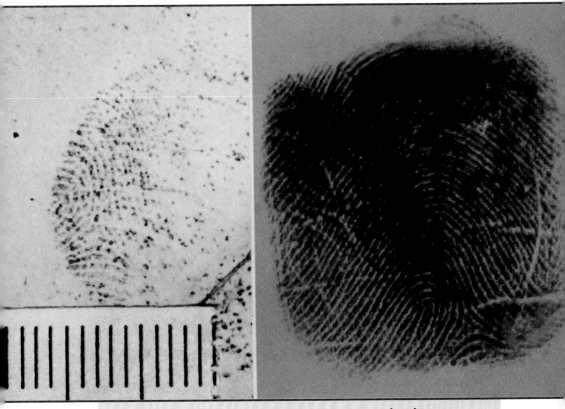

A partial fingerprint retrieved from a crime scene (*left*) being compared to a full fingerprint from a database. The red dots show the positions of distinguishing features on both, showing that the partial fingerprint is from the same finger as the print on file. *Philippe Psaila/Photo Researchers, Inc.*

works best on smooth, non-porous surfaces such as glass, polyethylene, and magazine paper, it can also be used on paper towels and even tissues. The beauty of VMD lies in the fact that prints are developed by using the smallest of materials, the atom. This provides the highest resolution and is able to produce marks with the best quality on both new and old samples. Critically, VMD is able to recover marks with only trace amounts of the substances that comprise every print.

The sample is placed in the top of a small decompression chamber. A few milligrams of gold are then laid in metal containers on the floor of the chamber. Once the chamber is sealed, the air is pumped out and a vacuum is created. The gold is then heated until it melts. As the fumes rise, they condense on the surface of the sample in an exceedingly fine layer—only one atom in depth. If no print is present, the layer will be uniform; but if a print is found, the gold will sink into its valleys, leaving the oily ridges uncoated.

This process is then repeated with a few milligrams of zinc. Like the gold, the zinc vaporizes inside the chamber, but its chemical properties mean that it only condenses onto other metals; therefore it sticks to the previous layer of gold. Because zinc won't adhere to any oily ridge, a high-contrast negative fingerprint is developed.

Of course a fingerprint is potentially worthless unless it can be linked either to a suspect or a database entry. This used to

## ♀ HISTORY IS MADE

The first killer to be caught using fingerprint evidence was an Argentinean woman named Francesca Rojas in 1892. She claimed that a local man who suffered from mental illness had burst into her home in Necochea on the Atlantic coastline and murdered her two children. The man was promptly arrested.

It looked like an open and shut case, but heading the Bureau of Identification at the regional headquarters at La Plata was a fingerprinting pioneer named Juan Vucetich. He dispatched Inspector Eduardo Alvarez to reinvestigate the crime.

Alvarez was appalled by the sloppiness of the original investigation. For instance, he found that the accused man had an unshakable alibi, but had been too mentally confused to mention it.

When Alvarez visited the crime scene, he found a bloody thumbprint. He recalled a recent lecture in which Vucetich had demonstrated the value of fingerprinting. Could that help? When Alvarez compared the bloody print to Rojas's, he saw that it matched perfectly. Confronted by the evidence of her own hand, Rojas confessed and was sentenced to life imprisonment.

mean long hours of poring over card indexes. Computerization has changed all that. The Integrated Automated Fingerprint Identification System (IAFIS), operated by the FBI, contains a huge and ever-expanding database of fingerprint records, and what once may have taken weeks or even months is now accomplished in seconds. The FBI program has proved so successful that most states and large urban jurisdictions now have AFIS systems of their own. This has led to many old crimes—some going back as far as 20 years—being solved using AFIS.

Each fingerprint is unique. They develop on a fetus at about six months and remain unchanged until the body decomposes after death. When one considers the vast array of physical changes that a human body will experience during its lifetime, this constancy at the tips of the fingers is truly remarkable. Although fingerprint individuality had been suspected since biblical times, it was Czechoslovakian physiologist Johannes Evangelista Purkinje (1787–1869) who first recognized and described nine basic patterns of fingerprints. The earliest practical application of fingerprints as a means of identification came in 1858, when a young administrative officer in India, William Herschel, adopted the local Bengali practice whereby illiterate workers "signed" for pay by leaving a thumbprint. This was done to help stamp out pension fraud. (Some wily ex-soldiers had taken to doubling their pensions by scribbling a mark when they were paid, then rejoining the line at the back and being paid out all over again.) As soon as Herschel made a record of each pensioner's fingerprints, the scam stopped overnight. Convinced that fingerprints could be a worthwhile aid in the business of identifying criminals, Herschel approached the local Inspector General of Prisons, only to be snubbed. Disillusioned, he returned to England in 1879.

That same year, a Scottish physician working in Japan, Henry Faulds, became involved in what is generally considered to be the first crime solved through the use of fingerprints. A burglar making his escape from a Tokyo house had left a dirty handprint on a whitewashed wall. When the police quickly arrested a suspect, Faulds inspected the man's prints and declared him wholly innocent, much to the amusement of skeptical investigators. Three days later Faulds was vindicated. Not only did another felon admit to the burglary, but his handprint also matched exactly the one

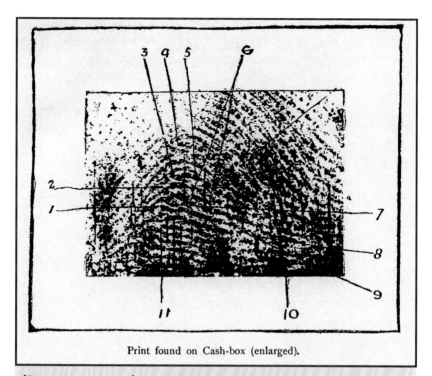

Print found on Cash-box (enlarged).

[This page and next] This example from Henry Faulds's *Guide to Finger-print Identification* (1905) shows fingerprint evidence from the 1905 Deptford Mask Murder Case. Following the murder of art shop manager Thomas Farrow, Albert Stratton was connected with the murder scene due to a fingerprint left on the shop's cash box [left] that matched his own [right]. Albert and his brother, Alfred, were later found guilty of murder and hanged. *Sheila Terry/Photo Researchers, Inc.*

left on the wall. Eagerly, Faulds published his findings in *Nature*, the British scientific journal, in 1880, sparking a long-running feud with Herschel, who still regarded himself as the father of fingerprinting.

It took another English scientist, Sir Francis Galton, to turn theory into practical reality. He laid out the ground rules for a basic classification system, putting the most commonly observed features into three groups—arches, loops, and whorls. His monumental work, *Finger Prints* (1892), lit the beacon, but it was left to yet

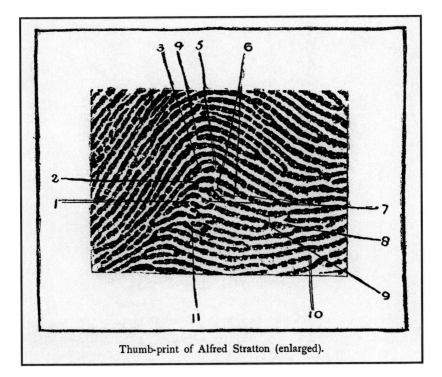

Thumb-print of Alfred Stratton (enlarged).

another Indian police officer, Edward Henry, to complete the task of classification.

In recent years, following a series of blunders on both sides of the Atlantic, the accuracy of fingerprinting has been under siege. Despite attempts by various courts to clarify what constitutes "scientific evidence," most notably in *Frye v. U.S 54 App. D. C. 46, 293 F. 1013* (1923) and *Daubert v. Merrell Dow Pharmaceuticals 113 S. Ct. 2786* (1993), the scientific basis for fingerprint identification remains tantalizingly elusive. All the recent fiascoes concern misidentification, usually of blurred or partial prints. Clear prints provide clear results. And those results, gleaned from more than 100 years of use, demonstrate that no two people have ever shared the same fingerprints.

# Identification of Remains:
## Buck Ruxton, 1935

Whenever a body is discovered the first question asked by any investigating officer is, "Who is it?" Because the majority of murder victims are killed by people they know, the answer to such a question can often lead directly to the killer, and it is for this reason that some murderers go to quite extraordinary lengths in order to conceal their victim's identity. Fortunately, dead bodies are extraordinarily difficult to dispose of: they are bulky and cumbersome, they tend to float in water, resist fire, smell awful, and, if left intact, are often jam-packed with clues to the owner's identity, in the form of fingerprints, DNA, and with increasing frequency, dental records. But it wasn't always so easy. At one time a dismembered corpse could pose enormous difficulties to even the most skilled pathologist. But science progresses and the killer's escape routes get closed off. A considerable number of escape routes were sealed off forever in the aftermath of the following remarkable case.

On the morning of September 29, 1935, a young woman crossing a bridge near Moffat, Scotland, glanced down at the River Annan below and spotted numerous parcels, some wrapped in newspaper, littering the bank. Protruding from one was a human arm. And it got much worse. From a huge crime scene search that stretched half a mile along both sides of the riverbank, investigators recovered 70 pieces of human remains, including two mutilated heads. Every item was taken to Edinburgh for analysis.

This spot, marked with a cross, is where searchers found the remains of the dismembered bodies of Isabella Van Ess and Mary Jane Rogerson in Dumfriesshire, Scotland, in September 1935. *AP*

The three pathologists charged with piecing together this grisly jigsaw puzzle—professors John Glaister, Sydney Smith, and J.C. Brash—agreed that whoever performed the dismemberment had done so with a high degree of anatomical skill and considerable patience. They estimated that the dissection had taken eight hours to complete. All the customary identifying marks—sex organs, fingertips, and facial features—had either been obliterated or were missing. One head was definitely female. The other skull appeared to be male, but the mutilation made identification almost impossible. It was this confusion that prompted initial newspaper reports to list the victims as a woman aged approximately 21 years old and about 5'1" tall, and a male of about 5'6" in height.

There were two strong indicators to suggest when the remains had been dumped in the gully through which the Annan flowed. It could not have been before September 15 because that was the date of one newspaper wrapped around the remains, while the discovery of body parts washed several hundred yards downstream suggested a date no later than September 19, when the Annan had flooded following heavy rain. For this reason, police concentrated their inquiries on anyone reported missing in the week immediately prior to September 19.

By chance, a local police officer had read a recent newspaper account of the disappearance from Lancaster—100 miles to the south—of a Mary Jane Rogerson, a maid at the home of Dr. Buck Ruxton. Inquiries revealed that Ruxton's wife had also disappeared at about the same time. This news prompted a re-examination of the supposedly male bones to determine if they could be those of a strongly built female.

Ruxton, an Indian-born doctor, and Isabella Van Ess, although never legally married, lived together as man and wife and had three children. Their relationship was stormy and violent. The Lancaster police were frequent callers to the Ruxton household, summoned to intervene in fights between the couple, mostly sparked by Ruxton's insane jealousy. Neither Isabella nor Mary Jane Rogerson had been seen since September 14, 1935, and since that time Ruxton had been acting like a madman. He had blurted out a string of stories—none convincing—to explain the dual disappearance, and he had bombarded weary police officers with demands that they search his home so that he might quash the vicious rumors circulating that he had done away with both wife and maid. At first the police had dismissed Ruxton as a crank; now they weren't so sure.

North of the border, investigators had made a breakthrough. One of the newspapers used to wrap the remains was a torn copy of the *Sunday Graphic*, dated September 15. A fragment of the paper showed a partial headline that read "—AMBE'S CARNIVAL QUEEN —ROWNED." Next to this was a photo of a young woman wearing a crown. The newspaper's circulation desk confirmed that this copy was a special regional edition, one sold only in the vicinity of Morecambe and Lancaster. Ominously, a Lancaster newsdealer confirmed that a *Sunday Graphic* had been delivered to the Ruxton household on September 15. Another clue came from a pair of rompers that had been wrapped around other body parts. A

Buck Ruxton, who was convicted of the murder of Isabella Van Ess and his housemaid, Mary Jane Rogerson, in a 1935 photo. Ruxton was hanged for the murders at Strangeways Prison in May 1936. *Topical Press Agency/Getty Images*

Lancaster woman identified them as a pair she had given to Mary Rogerson's mother to deliver to the Ruxton children.

Finally the police acceded to Ruxton's demand that they search his home at 2 Dalton Square. Despite evidence of a lengthy and exhaustive clean-up, bloodstains were everywhere, while the drains contained unmistakable traces of human fat. Ruxton's bluff had failed and, on October 13, he was formally charged with murder.

Meanwhile, the pathologists continued their labors. They assembled the skulls, torsos, 17 parts of limbs, and 43 portions of soft tissue into something resembling two human forms. In shape and size, the first body matched that of Mary Rogerson. The bones and teeth indicated a woman approximately 20 years old, Mary's age exactly. Also, plaster casts made of the feet fitted exactly into shoes known to have been worn by Mary. Closer examination of the second body suggested a woman between 35 and 45 years old; Isabella was 34 at the time of her disappearance.

Curiously, it was what the pathologists *didn't* find that provided the most convincing evidence of identification. The killer had deliberately removed certain distinguishing features from each body. For instance, Mary was known to suffer from a squint; the eyes in the first body had been removed from their sockets. Also the skin on the right upper arm had been scraped away, right in the area where Mary had a prominent birthmark. Similar disfigurement covered the spot where Mary's appendix scar would have shown. Likewise, at the base of her thumb where an old injury had left a scar, that area, too, had been shaved of tissue. But the clinching evidence came when, after hours of meticulous, often-frustrating effort, experts finally managed to take a single thumbprint from the decomposed flesh of the first body. It matched prints found at Dalton Square on articles habitually handled by Mary Rogerson. Just about the only thing that the pathologists couldn't ascertain was the actual cause of death; the mutilation was too thorough.

Examination of the second body was equally illuminating. Over half the teeth had obviously been extracted for some time, but the 14 remaining teeth had been wrenched out at around the time of death; and the nose was missing completely. Isabella Ruxton had very prominent teeth and a large nose. Also, her legs from knee to ankle were conspicuously of the same thickness: on the second body the legs had been pared of all flesh. The cause of death here,

An entomology doctoral student checks a colony of blow fly maggots feeding on calf liver in a study of the maggots' growth rate at various temperatures. The research could help murder investigations because experts can estimate a person's time of death by examining maggots found on the body. The study of the life cycle of maggots was able to aid the investigation of the murders of Isabella Van Ess and Mary Jane Rogerson in 1935 by determining the approximate time of death. *AP/University of Florida/IFAS, Thomas Wright*

though, was not in dispute. Congestion of the lungs and tongue pointed to asphyxiation, while a fractured hyoid—a tiny bone in the throat—confirmed that she had been strangled. Interestingly, the eyes, nose, ears, lips, and the tips of the fingers—all areas in which signs of asphyxia are found—had been removed, again adding to suspicions that the murderer had specialized medical knowledge.

However, conclusive proof that this was Isabella Ruxton came via a major forensic breakthrough. For the first time the photograph of a victim was superimposed over the skull to see if it would match. It fitted perfectly. Between them, the trio of Glaister, Smith, and Brash had slotted the final piece into an astonishing forensic jigsaw.

And there was more to come. Dr. Alexander Mearns of Glasgow University, in a pioneering feat of medical detection, by studying the life cycle of the maggots that infested the human remains, was able to establish that the victims were killed at about the time that Isabella Van Ess and Mary Jane Rogerson were last seen alive.

Ruxton was duly convicted and sentenced to death. Followi ng his execution on May 12, 1936, a newspaper printed a signed confession made by him, in which he admitted killing Isabella in a jealous fury, only to be interrupted by the unfortunate Mary Jane. As a witness, she, too, had to die.

There are 206 bones that make up the human skeleton. In the average male these bones weigh 12 pounds; for females, it is a couple of pounds less. To the trained eye, they form an illuminating guide to the body they inhabit. They can indicate how that person lived, any debilitating illnesses such as rickets or polio, healed fractures, whether that person was right- or left-handed, even possible clues as to occupation (for instance, waitresses show signs of arm strength in their bones, their strong side being more developed than the other side).

Basic questions arising from the discovery of any skeletal remains are:

1. *What was the person's age at the time of death?* Two features— the long bones and the skull—provide the best indicators. In infancy, the ends of the long bones are attached to the main shaft by cartilage. Gradually this cartilage ossifies and the two pieces of bone fuse together, a process that is usually complete by age 30. The varying stages of fusion can give an indication of age that is accurate to within two or three years. After age

30, these changes are more unreliable, with an accuracy of no better than plus or minus 10 years. The second indicator—skull changes—is also more detectable in childhood. The infant skull is made up of sections, marked by sutures that close up in stages. The frontal suture is the first to close, usually early in life. Other sutures normally close between the ages of 20 and 30, but some can remain open or only partially closed until age 60, making this form of age estimation progressively imprecise in later life.

2. *What was the sex of the skeleton?* The clearest indicators are the skull and the pelvis. The male skull is bulkier in many regions, while the female pelvis is much broader and shallower than that of the male.

3. *What was the person's race?* Using variation in eye socket shape and the nose, forensic anthropologists categorize people in one of three racial groups: Mongoloid (Asian), Negroid (African), and Caucasoid (European). In Negroids and Mongoloids the ridge of the nose is often broad in relation to height; in Caucasoids it is narrower.

In the Ruxton case, there was strong circumstantial evidence to suggest how long the bodies had lain by the river before they were found, but it's not always that straightforward. At the Anthropological Research Facility at the University of Tennessee in Knoxville, research is underway to quantify the effect of environmental factors on a dead body. The facility was founded in 1981 by Dr. William M. Bass as an outdoor laboratory with one specific aim—to scientifically document the timing of post-mortem decomposition. Known locally as "The Body Farm," and surrounded by razor wire, the facility has, at any one time, dozens of corpses dotted about its two and a half acres.

The corpses arrive and are placed in a variety of locations: car trunks, under canvas or plastic, buried in shallow graves, covered with brush, or submerged in ponds. The newly dead may lie alongside piles of disintegrating bones. They are exposed to wide extremes of temperature, from being refrigerated in total darkness, all the way to being left in sweltering summer sunlight. Then they are studied.

When a person dies, the body starts to decay immediately as enzymes in the digestive system begin eating the tissue. Then the insects and the climate take control. Attracted by the smell of putrefaction, blowflies begin their ravages, followed by small rodents and other animals. In hot weather total decomposition can be astonishingly fast. At the height of summer, for example, a body can deteriorate from fully intact to bare bones in just two weeks.

## ♀ DR. MILDRED TROTTER

Working out the height of an intact corpse is self-evident, although advanced decomposition can sometimes cloud the issue. What happens if a body or skeleton is incomplete? How then is the pathologist able to gauge how tall that person was? Fortunately, it is possible to arrive at a calculation thanks to a well-established relationship between the length of limbs and the total height of the body.

Much of the pioneering work in this field was conducted by Dr. Mildred Trotter (1899–1991), professor of anatomy at Washington University in St. Louis. In 1948–49, Trotter took a leave of absence from WU to join the Central Identification Laboratory for the U.S. Armed Forces in Hawaii, where she helped to repatriate the remains of servicemen killed in the Pacific combat of World War II. By studying the long bones of hundreds of servicemen, she and a statistician, Dr. Goldine Gleser, were able to calculate a height formula that is generally accurate to within plus or minus three centimeters. For a male Caucasoid the formula is:

Length of femur (thigh) x 2.38 + 61.41 cms = height
Length of tibia (shin) x 2.52 + 78.62 cms = height
Length of fibula (calf) x 2.68 + 71.78 cms = height

Additional tables that attempt to provide some indication of the corpse's build (that is, slender, medium, or heavy) are also employed. The most practical application for these calculations has been in the area of passenger identification after airline disasters or terrorist action.

Professor Trotter's remarkable work continued up to the day before her 86th birthday, when she was disabled by a stroke. In accordance with her wishes, upon her death on August 23, 1991, her body was donated to the Washington School of Medicine.

Each stage of decomposition is recorded and analyzed, then added to the growing databank that is made available to law enforcement agencies. Sometimes attempts are made to duplicate the circumstances of a particular crime, but primarily the research is targeted toward gathering data that might assist in future cases.

Close attention is also paid to soil samples because bodies leak fatty acids into the ground beneath them as they decompose. Analysis of this soil can help to determine how long a body was lying in a particular area, or whether it was first placed somewhere else and then later moved to its present location. Soil analysis can also reveal the presence of a corpse, even if the body itself has been removed or destroyed. The "stain" left by the fatty acids, which also affects plant life around it, can last as long as two years, leaving a kind of phantom fingerprint in the earth.

A similar research facility exists in North Carolina, and authorities hope more such facilities will be established across the United States. This is necessary to study the effect of regional variations in climate. For example, a body subjected to a winter in Montana would yield significantly different data to that of one left in Florida at the same time of year.

# Questioned Documents:
## Angelo John LaMarca, 1956

The questioned documents examiner needs to wear many hats. Mastery of the discipline requires knowledge of ink, paper, and typography, the sequence of events involved in the preparation and handling of a document, the alteration of a document, and its age. Underpinning everything else is the examination of handwriting with the intention of ascertaining authorship of a document. Generally, handwriting experts are called on in cases of forgery—a disputed will, perhaps—but occasionally they do figure prominently in other crimes as well.

On July 4, 1956, little Peter Weinberger was kidnapped from the patio of his home at Westbury, Long Island. He was just one month old. His mother, Beatrice, had left him for just a minute as she stepped indoors to fetch a diaper. When she returned the carriage was empty. Lying on the patio floor was a ransom note. Written in green ink, with skillful and highly singular penmanship, on a sheet torn from a student notebook, it read:

"Attention.

I am sorry this had to happen, but I am in bad need of money & couldn't get it any other way.

Don't tell anyone or go to the Police about this, because I am watching you closely. I am scared stiff & will kill the baby, at your first wrong move.

Just put $2,000 $^{00}$/xxx (Two thousand) in small bills in a brown envelope & place it next to the sign Post at the corner of Albemarle Rd. and Park Ave. at <u>Exactly</u> 10 o'clock tomorrow (Thursday) morning. If everything goes smooth, I will bring the baby back & leave him on the same corner "Safe & Happy" at exactly 12 noon.

No excuses. I can't wait!

Your baby sitter."[1]

Despite the warning, the Weinbergers immediately contacted the Nassau County police, and that same day details of the kidnapping reached the Federal Bureau of Investigation's New York office. Although FBI agents were dispatched to the scene, their hands were tied. Because no evidence existed to show that Peter had been transported across a state line or that the kidnapper had used interstate communications, federal law mandated that jurisdiction remained with the local police. FBI frustration only intensified when a New York daily newspaper snubbed requests for a media blackout and reported details of the ransom note before its demands were fulfilled. This had disastrous repercussions. When Mrs. Weinberger arrived at the drop-off spot with the ransom, she was swamped by hordes of reporters. The drop-off degenerated into a fiasco and Bertha Weinberger went home without her baby.

On July 10 the kidnapper twice telephoned the Weinbergers to reiterate his demands and a second drop was arranged. Once again there was no sign of Peter Weinberger. A search of the drop-off zone did, however, reveal a bag that contained a further note from the kidnapper. Penned on the back of an order form later traced to the Dynalum Window Products Company in Garden City, Long Island, it read:

"If everything goes smooth the baby will be left wraped [sic] in a Army blanket & placed at the exit of the Parkway closest to your house in exactly 1 hour.

Your baby sitter."[2]

Baby Peter Weinberger was kidnapped from this house by Angelo John LaMarca on July 4, 1956. *Pete Stackpole/Getty Images*

The next day FBI agents officially entered the case under the provisions of the Lindbergh Kidnapping Law (1934), which stated that after seven days a presumption could be made that a kidnap victim had been transported across state lines.

Apart from the taped telephone calls, the best hope of identifying the kidnapper lay with the extortion notes. FBI handwriting experts, drafted into the investigation headquarters at Mineola, Long Island, found distinguishing characteristics in 16 letters of the alphabet. Most noticeable was the manner in which the kidnapper's lowercase script *m* resembled a sideways *z*.

Such stylistic quirks convinced investigators that if the kidnapper had ever filled in an official form, they would be able to pinpoint his handwriting. With this in mind, they began a search of all local records. It started with fingerprint cards and files from the Long Island police, and then widened to include handwriting specimens from automobile registration forms, post office files, voter registrations, hospital records, every conceivable place where handwriting was used. Whenever a signature or a piece of writing that even remotely resembled the distinctive ransom demands was found, it was sent to Mineola for closer examination.

After seven weeks of mind-numbing drudgery and almost two million handwriting samples, on August 22 an FBI agent at the Brooklyn Probation and Parole Bureau wearily picked up a probation violation form filled out by Angelo John LaMarca, 31, who had been arrested in a 1954 raid on a small-time bootlegging operation. LaMarca had received a 90-day suspended sentence and probation. Significantly, on July 5—one day after the kidnapping—he had failed to report to his probation officer and did not show up until July 28, at which time he filled out the required form to explain his absence. The agent studied LaMarca's handwriting closely; even to his untrained eye, it closely resembled that on the ransom notes. The probation report was rushed to Mineola, where experts led by Dr. Fred M. Miller pored over LaMarca's handwriting and made a positive identification. It was the 1,974,545th piece of handwriting they had compared.

At 2:15 a.m. on August 23 LaMarca, an auto-mechanic with heavy debts, was arrested at his home in Plainview, just a few miles from the Weinberger residence. At first he denied any involvement, but after being shown the handwriting evidence he confessed. He explained that he had taken the baby to the designated meeting place, only to be scared off by the reporters. Panic-stricken, he had abandoned the infant, leaving him alive in some heavy brush near Exit 37 of Northern State Parkway near Plainview. On August 24, the decomposed remains of Peter Weinberger were found in the thicket LaMarca had described. The baby had perished from starvation and exposure.

At the garage where LaMarca worked, agents found a pad of order blanks imprinted with the name of the same window products company found on the second ransom note. Microscopic examination showed that the same paper cutter had trimmed both pad and note, leaving its telltale markings on the edges of the paper.

LaMarca was convicted of first-degree murder and kidnapping and sentenced to death. After several stays of execution, he finally went to the electric chair on August 7, 1958. In the aftermath of this tragedy Congress changed the federal kidnapping laws, authorizing the FBI to enter abduction cases after just 24 hours rather than having to wait seven days.

Like all other evidence, handwriting is identified on the basis of individuality. Children may be taught a specific way of forming letters, but from an early age they begin to inject their own quirks and idiosyncrasies. By the time a person reaches maturity, so the theory goes, their writing has acquired sufficient peculiarities to identify them.

Unfortunately it's not that straightforward. In truth, one's handwriting is constantly changing. Fluctuations can occur, often from day-to-day. Mood, the position in which one sits, one's physical

## ⚲ THE OSBORN FAMILY

America's pioneering handwriting expert was Michigan-born Albert S. Osborn (1858–1946), whose *Questioned Documents* (1910) and *The Problem of Proof* (1922) quickly became recognized texts on the subject, cited and acknowledged in courtrooms everywhere. During a long career—it lasted almost 40 years and he testified in 39 states—Osborn was featured in many famous cases, among them the second murder trial of Roland B. Molineaux (1902), a New York socialite who had been accused of mailing a package of poisoned medication to a hated rival. (The rival escaped unharmed, but his housekeeper swallowed a dose of the medicine and died in agony.) But his most famous case was the Lindbergh kidnapping-murder. In 1927 Charles Lindbergh gained worldwide fame when he became the first person to fly the Atlantic solo. On March 1, 1932, his baby son, Charles Jr., was kidnapped. A string of ransom notes demanding $50,0000 were sent to the Lindberghs, but on May 12 the baby was found dead about two miles from the family home. Osborn was called in and asked to cast his expert eye over the ransom notes.

well-being, all these can affect the way someone puts pen to paper. However, to the skilled examiner, there is, beneath these superficial deviations, a unique style that shines through, defying any attempt at disguise. It might be the angle of writing, its uniformity across the page, or the manner in which letters are formed, such as whether letters like *g* and *h* are looped or not. Such analysis requires vast experience and a large investment of time before a considered opinion can be given.

A forged signature presents very specific problems. Phony signatures based upon memory tend to contain a combination of the forger's own writing habits and his or her recollection of the victim's habits. In these instances, the discrepancies are often obvious. If, however, the perpetrator makes a careful drawing of the victim's signature or traces an authentic signature, while the forgery may be exposed, identifying the perpetrator is next to impossible, since two individuals making careful tracings of the same signature can produce virtually identical drawings.

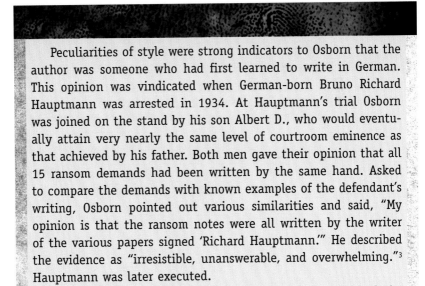

Peculiarities of style were strong indicators to Osborn that the author was someone who had first learned to write in German. This opinion was vindicated when German-born Bruno Richard Hauptmann was arrested in 1934. At Hauptmann's trial Osborn was joined on the stand by his son Albert D., who would eventually attain very nearly the same level of courtroom eminence as that achieved by his father. Both men gave their opinion that all 15 ransom demands had been written by the same hand. Asked to compare the demands with known examples of the defendant's writing, Osborn pointed out various similarities and said, "My opinion is that the ransom notes were all written by the writer of the various papers signed 'Richard Hauptmann.'" He described the evidence as "irresistible, unanswerable, and overwhelming."[3] Hauptmann was later executed.

In 1942 Osborn founded, and became the first president of, the American Society of Questioned Document Examiners. It remains the foremost organization of its type in the world.

Handwriting expert James Clark Sellers points to two signatures in an evidence exhibit for the trial of Bruno Hauptmann for the kidnapping of the Lindbergh baby. Sellers testified that Hauptmann's signature [top] matched the handwriting on the ransom notes [bottom]. A similar use of handwriting analysis was vital in the prosecution of Angelo John LaMarca. *Bettmann/Corbis*

Besides handwriting analysis, the questioned documents examiner is frequently called upon to identify a source of mechanical writing. In the past this usually meant a typewriter. Here, reference files and differentiation charts hold the key, listing, as they do, every kind of typeface design. A specific typewriter could be identified if it contained sufficient individuality, based on broken or tilting characters, badly aligned characters, characters that print more heavily on one side than on another, and characters that don't always strike the page evenly. Since it is impossible to reinsert a document into a typewriter in its exact former position, it is possible, using a ruled screen, to determine if a document has been prepared at one sitting or has been reinserted. (Nowadays, of course, printers and copiers are the norm, and how these may be identified will be explained later.)

Building on this mechanical expertise, the examiner also needs to have knowledge of the history of print technology. Say, for example, a document was purportedly written in 1912 yet records showed that the machine upon which it was typed was not manufactured until 1938, then that document must be viewed with the utmost skepticism.

Other factors to be considered are ink and paper. In the 1920s the American Secret Service acquired the International Ink Library from the police in Zurich, Switzerland. Nowadays, the library contains the chemical composition and other information, such as date of formulation, on more than 7,000 types of ink. The library also maintains a watermark collection of more than 22,000 images, as well as collections of plastics, toners, and computer printer inks. Although ink comparisons may provide invaluable evidence, it is not possible to individualize ink; that is, identify it as coming from a unique source.

Papers can be identified on the basis of fiber, filler, and sizing constituents (the ingredients that apply a smooth film to the paper). Fibers can be identified by microscopic examination and differential staining (a process of using various dyes to establish the components). Fillers, because they are crystalline substances, can be identified by the way they scatter X-rays. Sizing constituents are readily identified by chemical tests.

Determining whether a document has been altered is usually possible through electrostatic detection apparatus (ESDA), which seeks out indentations. The document is placed on top of an electronically charged metal mesh and a thin plastic film is pulled tightly across it. An electrostatic charge is then applied to the film. As the document and the film are sucked tight onto the mesh, an oppositely charged black toner is applied, which clings to the indentations. When the original document is removed, the indentations on the film may be read. By matching all suspect original pages against each image, investigators can determine whether changes have been made.

Research published by a Secret Service study[4] suggests that ESDA may also be able to help identify printers. Instead of concentrating on the characters, it looks for indentations made by the paper-feeding mechanism or some other part of the printer hardware. The principle is similar to that of the rifled gun barrel (see Chapter 5) with minute variations in the manufacturing process ensuring that each printer will leave its own identifiable marks on a sheet of paper.

Questions concerning the sequence of writing can be vital in proving the authenticity of a document. For example, it may be necessary to determine whether or not the ink signature is over or under the typewritten portion of a document. In this and related problems, such as deciphering and restoration of eradicated or erased writing, most examinations today are carried out primarily using computer-based technology.

One of the most powerful additions to the questioned documents examiner's arsenal is the Video Spectral Comparator 2000 (VSC2000), a sophisticated imaging device that allows an examiner to analyze inks, visualize hidden security features, and reveal alterations on a document. Using the VSC2000's infrared radiant energy source and filters, the examiner is able to see through inks to reveal objects that are obscured to the naked eye. But it has other uses.

For instance, the specimen can be subjected to a variety of light sources while cameras and filters record the effect on a visual display unit (VDU). Software enables the examiner to manipulate the image for easier viewing. Images can be overlaid or compared side by side—useful in performing torn edge comparisons on sheets of paper—and they can determine whether a page has been added or replaced in a multipage contract. The VSC2000 can even aid the examiner to sort shredded pieces of paper, allowing the reconstruction of a readable document.

# Offender Profiling:
# George Metesky, 1957

Of all the investigative disciplines used by law enforcement, probably nothing has attracted so much media hype or controversy as offender profiling. When depicted on TV, it looks miraculous; an earnest-looking psychologist studies a crime scene, takes a few notes, consults a database or two, and then astonishes an awestruck audience of detectives with a dazzling solution to their problems. In the real world it's very different. Here, offender profiling is still struggling to find its place. The problem is one of status: there is nothing remotely scientific about offender profiling; it's all a question of interpretation.

Although similar complaints have recently been leveled against fingerprinting, at least with a print there is a visible piece of evidence to discuss. The criminal profiler has no such luxury. His job is to get inside the head of the perpetrator. Thus far, the judicial system has been decidedly cool toward offender profiling. Every attempt to have profiles admitted as "evidence" *per se* has been quashed by the courts. But this isn't to say that profiling doesn't have its uses, even if it rarely scales the heights achieved in the following famous case.

Between 1940 and 1956 New Yorkers were targeted with a series of explosions by someone who became known as the "Mad Bomber." The campaign of terror was punctuated by an oddly worded series of letters in which the bomber bitterly attacked Consolidated Edison, better known as ConEd, the company that supplies New York City with its electricity.

On December 2, 1956, the biggest bomb to date exploded in Brooklyn's Paramount Theater, injuring six people. Following this, psychiatrist Dr. James A. Brussel was asked to study the bomber's letters, and to draw up a profile of the likely writer. Newspaper accounts of Brussel's profile, published on December 25, 1956, varied in several details, but in essence it was as follows:

Single man, between 40 and 50 years old, introvert. Well-proportioned in build. He's single, a loner, perhaps living with an older, female relative. He is very neat, tidy, and clean-shaven. Good education, but of foreign extraction. Skilled mechanic, neat with tools. Not interested in women. He's a Slav. Religious. Might flare up violently at work when criticized. Possible motive: discharge or reprimand. Feels superior to his critics. Resentment keeps growing. His letters are posted from Westchester, and he wouldn't be stupid enough to post them from where he lives. He probably mails the letters between his home and New York City. There is a large concentration of Slavs in Connecticut, and to get from there to New York you have to pass through Westchester. He has had a bad disease—possibly heart trouble. Present or former Consolidated Edison worker.

As an afterthought Brussel added: "When you catch him he'll be wearing a double-breasted suit—buttoned."

Brussel's profile received enormous media coverage, with newspapers urging the Bomber to contact them. He swallowed the bait. In his next three letters the Bomber finally divulged the reason for his campaign: a failure to win redress for injuries he had allegedly sustained while working for ConEd.

But ConEd was already one step ahead of their tormentor. Brussel's belief that the Bomber had at one time been a ConEd employee had prompted a renewed search of the company's archives. Originally it was thought that all employee records prior to 1940 had been destroyed, but on January 14, 1957, a new cache was found. The very next day a clerk named Alice G. Kelly was leafing through these documents when her eyes fell upon the employment record of a George P. Metesky, who, in September 1931, had been injured in an industrial accident. A lengthy legal battle for compensation had ended with Metesky having all his claims against the company

George Metesky (*center*), wearing the buttoned double-breasted suit that profiler Dr. James Brussel predicted, is surrounded by police as he is booked at the Waterbury Police Station in January 1957.
*Bettmann/Corbis*

This January 1957 photo shows the garage where George Metesky made his bombs. *Time & Life Pictures/Getty Images*

dismissed. Miss Kelly, who had followed the Mad Bomber case closely, read through Metesky's letters of complaint, and she was struck by his tortured syntax and odd phraseology. It all seemed eerily similar to the style of writing used by the Mad Bomber. Plucking the file out from the rest, she turned to her supervisor and said, "I think I have it."[1] The supervisor agreed and the police were informed immediately.

Detectives who rushed to Metesky's home in Waterbury, Connecticut, in the middle of the night discovered a bomb-making workshop in the garage. They also found a man well-proportioned, aged 54, of Polish extraction, unmarried, and living in a house with two older sisters. When told to get dressed, Metesky went upstairs and returned wearing a double-breasted suit—buttoned! Metesky freely admitted being the Mad Bomber, and in April 1957 he was committed to Matteawan Hospital for the criminally insane.

Brussel modestly downplayed his astonishing triumph, attributing it to deductive reasoning, experience, and playing the percentages. His reasoning went as follows: because paranoia takes time to develop—often as long as 10 years—and the first bomb had been planted in 1940, he felt the man's illness would have started around

## ♀ PROBLEMS IN PROFILING

In almost every respect psychological profiling is far more entrenched—and certainly better organized and funded—in the United States than it is in Europe, where doubts persist. Critics highlight one spectacular British catastrophe in 1994 when the murder trial of Colin Stagg, accused of murdering a young woman named Rachel Nickell, was halted after the judge decided that there was not a shred of evidence to link the defendant to the crime except a highly tenuous profile. The profiler in question, who was perceived to be quarterbacking the entire investigation, was slammed by the judge as a "puppet master," who had overseen "a blatant attempt to incriminate a suspect by . . . deceptive conduct of the grossest kind."[2]

In 2002 the Washington, D.C., sniper case further fueled arguments that offender profiling still has some considerable distance to travel before it can ever fully enter the forensic science mainstream. During the investigation an army of experts flooded the airwaves on television and radio with a bewildering array of profiles that were not only wildly dissimilar, but were positively dangerous in the way that they diverted police resources. The snipers were ultimately arrested as a result of concrete police work and a tip from an alert citizen.

1930, making him middle-aged in 1956. Why a paranoid? Because, according to Brussel, they are the champion grudge-holders, are neat and obsessive, and tidy to a fault—hence the meticulous printing and the double-breasted suit.

Although the notes suggested an educated mind, they smacked of having been translated into English. Why a Slav? Because historically, bombs have been favored in Central Europe. Well-proportioned? In a broad-based study, German psychiatrist Ernst Kretschmer had demonstrated a correlation between a person's build, personality, and any mental illness that might develop. Kretschmer stated that 85 percent of paranoiacs have an athletic body build. Here, Brussel was going with the averages. (It should be noted that Kretschmer's theories are largely unsupported by empirical evidence.)

In fact, just about the only thing Brussel got wrong was the heart disease, but even there he didn't miss by much. Metesky actually suffered from a tubercular lung.

No modern profiler—outside the pages of fiction—would dare attempt anything so specific. Real-life offender profiling deals far more in generalities and is based on the principle that behind every criminal act is the criminal mind. Underpinning this concept is a belief that criminals leave psychological clues at the scene of the crime. By carefully sifting these clues, a skilled interpreter isolates those characteristics of the likely offender that separate them from the general population, gradually whittling down the list of potential suspects and allowing the investigative team to focus their efforts in the best possible area. Common sense, observation, background knowledge, and geographical considerations play as big a role in this process as does psychology, for only by studying all facets of the crime can the profiler hope to be successful.

The first in-depth analysis of the homicidal mind came in 1930 with Professor Karl Berg's study of the serial killer Peter Kürten, known as the "Monster of Dusseldorf." However, this was compiled while Kürten was awaiting execution and contributed nothing to his capture. Two years later a rudimentary attempt was made to profile the kidnapper of Charles Lindbergh, Jr., again with limited success. Profiling next surfaced in 1943 when U.S. intelligence agencies asked a Boston-based psychoanalyst, Walter C. Langer, to unravel the complexities of Adolf Hitler's mind. The hope was to gain insights into Hitler's future military strategy. Langer concluded that Hitler was delusional, a bully, incapable of close personal relationships, and would most likely commit suicide. Whether his profile contributed in any way to the outcome of the war is unknowable.

Thereafter the forensic examination of the human mind fell into disuse until Brussel's intervention in the Mad Bomber case. Another decade would pass before offender profiling again emerged from the shadows. This time the flag-bearer was Howard Teten, an agent at the FBI Academy in Quantico, Virginia. Primed by long consultations with Brussel, Teten started laying the groundwork for the first concerted attempt at predictive analysis of the criminal mind. In 1972 he was joined by Pat Mullany and, together, they established the FBI's Behavioral Science Unit (BSU) at Quantico.

Time and budgetary constraints limited the team to studying only the most serious crimes. This brought them face-to-face with some of America's worst serial killers: Charles Manson, Richard Speck, David Berkowitz, John Wayne Gacy, Ted Bundy, and others.

## ⚲ THE FBI'S BEHAVIORAL SCIENCE UNIT

In recent years the Behavioral Science Unit has diversified from its original role. It has become part of the FBI's training program, with a goal of training members of outside law enforcement agencies in the techniques and methods of the FBI. Although the teachers still include clinical forensic psychologists, students now receive instruction from specialists in the fields of research and management analysis, and technical information.

The focus is very much geared toward studying the offender and his or her behavioral patterns and motivations. In short, they want to know why people commit crimes. This has led the training program to widen its focus. Now, instead of concentrating solely on serial killers, it extends into all areas of crime, most notably terrorism and gang violence. Even something so seemingly removed as air-rage falls within the teaching curriculum.

Lessons learned at Quantico can apply to almost any serious crime situation.

Information gleaned from these interviews was entered on a computer database, and then scoured in an attempt to discover similar and repeatable behavior patterns. An early discovery was that most serial killers fall into one of two categories: organized and disorganized. The former are calculating and likely to plan their crimes, whereas disorganized killers are creatures of reflex, impulsive and senseless with little consideration for outcome or consequence.

As the profilers gained experience, they turned their attention more to crime scene analysis. They studied photographs, autopsy reports, witness statements, and, vitally, any evidence that was left at the crime scene. Factors to be considered included motive, mobility, victim preference, murder weapon, location, etc.

As its analysis became increasingly sophisticated, the FBI formed the National Center for the Analysis of Violent Crime (NCAVC) in 1984, and its offshoot, the Violent Criminal Apprehension Program (ViCAP), a nationwide attempt to systematically collate data related to crimes of violence. Cases typically examined by ViCAP include:

1. Solved or unsolved homicides, especially those that involve an abduction.
2. Murders that are apparently random, motiveless, or sexually oriented; or are known or suspected to be part of a series.
3. Missing persons, where the circumstances indicate a strong possibility of foul play and the victim is still missing.
4. Unidentified dead bodies where the manner of death is known or suspected to be homicide.

The ViCAP Crime Analysis Report contains no fewer than 189 questions, ranging from details of the crime and its victims, to the *modus operandi* (MO), autopsy data, and forensic evidence. Once this report has been completed by the investigating agency, ViCAP personnel can access it in the database, seeking out similarities to previous crimes, particularly if it appears as though these crimes may have been committed by the same offender. If patterns are found, the law enforcement agency involved will be notified.

The FBI's role in most cases is that of adviser. Actually solving a crime and apprehending the perpetrator is still the job of the investigating agency, such as a local police department. There are currently slightly more than 30 agents qualified to work on ViCAP, and each year they receive more than 1,000 profiling requests from law enforcement agencies, not only in America, but also around the globe.

By its very nature, psychological profiling tends to be retrospective, and while solutions to crimes of the present may be suggested by crimes of the past, the shrewd profiler is constantly aware that mankind's capacity for evil is as innovative as it is infinite.

# Firearms
# Examination:
## John Branion, 1967

No one knows for certain when human beings first began killing each other with firearms, but there is evidence to suggest that by 1364 the inhabitants of Perugia in modern-day Italy were already well versed in the handgun's destructive power.[1] From there, firearms swept across Europe, and they came with the first settlers to the United States. In 2004 there were 9,404 people shot to death feloniously in the United States.[2] This makes the role of the firearms examiner absolutely critical to the proper administration of justice. It is his or her job to match bullets to barrels, and to identify firearms. For this reason their knowledge of weapons needs to be encyclopedic, as the following case vividly demonstrates.

Just before lunch on December 22, 1967, Dr. John Branion, 41, set off in his car from the Ida Mae Scott Hospital on Chicago's south side. Several minutes later—after passing his home—he picked up his young son from nursery school, then he stopped at the home of Maxine Brown, who was scheduled to have lunch with the Branions that day. When Mrs. Brown decided not to have lunch, Branion drove to his apartment at 5054 South Woodlawn Avenue.

He arrived at 11:57 a.m. to find his wife, Donna, lying on the utility room floor. She had been shot several times. Branion immediately summoned help. A neighbor, Dr. Helen Payne, examined the stricken woman and confirmed the obvious: Donna Branion was dead.

When questioned, another neighbor, Theresa Kentra, reported hearing several muffled thuds and a commotion of some sort at approximately 11:30 a.m. She had thought no more of it until just before midday when she observed Branion coming out of his apartment. Although he was shouting for assistance, she noticed that "he did not seem upset."[3]

Officer Alvin Kerston, assigned to the mobile unit of the Chicago Police Department Crime Laboratory, searched the area around the body and recovered three expended bullets and four cartridge casings. Two pellets were under the body and one near it. A fourth, still in the victim's arm, was found during the autopsy.

The bullets that killed Donna Branion were .38 caliber and had red dots on the shell casing primers, typical of German-made Geco ammunition. Although this ammunition was quite common, microscopic examination revealed distinctive rifling patterns—six lands and grooves (explained later in this chapter), and a right twist. Also, the casings had marks on the base, a sign that the weapon used to fire them had a loading indicator (this lets the shooter know if a cartridge is inserted in the breech). Firearms expert Burt Nielsen knew of only one pistol that fulfilled all these criteria—a Walther PPK. When Branion, an avid gun collector, was asked if he owned any weapon capable of firing .38 caliber ammunition, he said only one, a Hi Standard. No mention was made of a Walther. Tests conducted on the Hi Standard eliminated it as the murder weapon.

Detectives were puzzled by the lack of apparent motive for the killing. There was no sign of a robbery, and Donna was not known to have any enemies except, possibly, her husband.

Neighborhood rumors hinted that the Branion marriage had been rocky. Branion did nothing to dampen the gossip when, just 48 hours after the tragedy, he flew to Colorado for a Christmas ski-vacation. While Branion enjoyed himself on the slopes, detectives in Chicago dug into his background. They learned that Branion was a notorious womanizer whose affairs had provoked numerous violent arguments with Donna.

Another troubling aspect was something Branion had said at the murder scene. He told officers that he had not bothered to examine his wife's body because he could tell from the lividity (discoloration of the skin due to blood settling) that she was dead. And yet, according to Dr. Payne, when she saw the body at just after midday, lividity was not visibly present. Upon his return from Colorado, Branion was quizzed about this discrepancy. He backtracked hastily, explaining that he had really meant to say "cyanosis," a bluish discoloration of the skin caused by de-oxygenated blood. Lividity, he said, had just been a slip of the tongue.

On January 22, 1968, Detective Michael Boyle returned to Branion's apartment with a search warrant. In a cabinet that had been locked on the day of the murder, he found a brochure for a Walther PPK, an extra clip, and a manufacturer's target, all bearing the serial number 188274. He also found two boxes of Geco-brand .38 caliber ammunition. One full box contained 25 shells; the other had four shells missing, the same number of shots that had killed Donna Branion.

The net began to close around Branion. Import records for Walther PPKs showed that model number 188274 was shipped to a Chicago store, where it had been purchased by William Hooks III, a friend of Branion's. Hooks admitted giving the gun to Branion as a birthday gift almost a year before the killing.

When confronted by this revelation, the doctor panicked. His original statement specifically mentioned that nothing had been stolen; now he blustered that the Walther and another gun had been taken by the intruders who killed his wife. One change of story too many, it led to Branion being charged with murder.

At his trial, prosecutors declared that the story Branion had told was correct in every respect save one—chronology. Yes, he had picked up his son and driven to Maxine Brown's, but first he had sneaked home and shot his wife. Joyce Kelly, a teacher at the nursery school, testified that Branion, normally so laid-back, had rushed in, flustered and panting for breath, between 11:45 a.m. and 11:50 a.m., some 10 minutes later than he had claimed.

But did Branion have sufficient time to commit the crime? Boyle described a series of tests that he and another officer had performed while driving the route allegedly taken by Branion. They had covered the 2.8-mile journey in a minimum of six minutes and a maximum of 12 minutes. Time enough, said the prosecution, for Branion to have committed the murder, picked up his son, and established an alibi. With that alibi in tatters and the damning firearms

# COMPARISON MICROSCOPE ON TRIAL

The comparison microscope's first crucial test came in the notorious Sacco and Vanzetti case. In 1921 two Italian-born laborers and political agitators, Nicola Sacco and Bartolomeo Vanzetti, were sentenced to death for killing two guards during a botched robbery the year before. Both men had loaded weapons in their possession at the time of arrest, and Sacco's was .32 caliber, the same as one of the murder bullets. Also, bullets used in the shooting—Peters, Winchester, and Remington—matched those found in Sacco's possession. The trial was dominated by firearms testimony, with defense experts adamant that Sacco's gun was not the murder weapon.

Skillful media manipulation turned Sacco and Vanzetti into left-wing martyrs, the victims of a government witch hunt. For six years the arguments raged. With the outcry at fever pitch, in June 1927, America's foremost firearms expert, Calvin Goddard, who worked alongside Philip O. Gravelle at the Bureau of Forensic Ballistics (BFB), was asked to adjudicate on the confusing ballistics testimony. Armed not only with the recently invented comparison microscope but also a helixometer—a hollow probe fitted with a light and a magnifying glass for examining the insides of gun barrels—Goddard resolved to settle the dispute once and for all.

With defense expert Augustus Gill acting as witness, Goddard fired a bullet from Sacco's revolver into cotton wool, then placed it beside the murder bullet on the comparison microscope. The outcome was unequivocal—the murder bullet had been fired from Sacco's Colt automatic. Gill, peering through the microscope, had to agree. When fellow defense expert James Burns also changed his opinion, Sacco and Vanzetti were doomed. On August 23, 1927, over worldwide protest, they died in the electric chair.

Two subsequent retests of the Colt pistol—the most recent in 1983—vindicated Goddard's pioneering use of the comparison microscope. Both confirmed that Sacco's weapon *had* been used in the murderous robbery.

evidence—although the Walther PPK was never found—Branion's fate was sealed. On May 28, 1968, Branion was convicted of murder and sentenced to a 20- to 30-year prison term.

He was released on a cash bond of just $500, pending appeal. In 1971, with his legal options expiring fast, Branion jumped bail and fled to Europe. After an amazing jaunt across two continents, he found asylum in Uganda, occasionally acting as personal physician to Idi Amin, that country's dictator. When Amin was toppled from power in 1979, the new government wanted nothing to do with Branion and the U.S. government began extradition proceedings. On October 15, 1983, Branion was returned in handcuffs to American soil and sent to Joliet State Prison.

In August 1990, Branion was released on grounds of poor health. One month later, at age 64, he died of a brain tumor and heart ailment.

Gunpowder is believed to have been introduced into Europe from Arabia in about 1300 A.D., and firearms followed shortly thereafter. But another two centuries would pass before the next great firearms milestone was reached. This came when engineers realized that by etching a spiral groove into the gun barrel—a process called rifling—they could impart spin to the projectile, and thereby vastly improve its accuracy.

After being smooth-bored, the gun barrel blank is reamed to specification diameter, and is then rifled. The raised parts of these rifling marks are called "lands" while the valleys are termed "grooves." Rifling not only enhanced the lethal nature of firearms, it also made them identifiable. Because the machine tools used to manufacture barrels wear minutely with each succeeding gun, this makes every gun barrel in the world unique. And this uniqueness is transferred in the form of distinctive scratch marks to each bullet that passes through that particular barrel.

The realization that rifling might assist in matching a bullet to a firearm took time to catch hold. In 1900 a groundbreaking article titled "The Missile and the Weapon" appeared in the *Buffalo Medical Journal*. Written by a New York physician named Dr. Albert Llewellyn Hall, it explored methods of systematically measuring land and groove markings on bullets, the examination of gunpowder residues in barrels of firearms, and the physical changes that take place over time after a weapon is fired. Although Hall did testify at several criminal trials in the early twentieth century, sadly, his pioneering work is little remembered today, and he remains one of the great, unsung heroes of firearms examination history.

Those who followed in his footsteps soon realized that other factors besides the barrel contribute to bullet individuality. When fired, a bullet is driven forward through the barrel; simultaneously, its shell casing hurtles back against the breech face. Any imperfection on that breech face will impress itself on the case head. Similarly, other parts of the gun mechanism such as the firing pin, the extractor, and the ejector post all may etch marks on the head or shell casing.

After exiting the muzzle, a bullet is affected by its surroundings. If it strikes human bone or any hard object severe distortion may result, making it difficult to conclusively identify its lands and grooves. For this reason, comparisons of casings from test firings taken from a crime scene often provide better results than comparisons of the bullets themselves.

The distance from which a weapon is fired often figures prominently in criminal cases. This can be determined up to several feet by examining various factors: the form and size of the bullet hole, the extent of burning around the hole, the amount of embedded powder grains, and the presence of mercury or lead from primers (substances that ignite the powder in a round). Such information can be vital in determining whether a gunshot wound was self-inflicted. Infrared, X-ray, and chemical tests are used to determine the extent of powder residues. If the firearm is available, another factor to consider in close contact wounds is the amount—if any—of human tissue in the barrel. Tests have established that the amount of human tissue or "blowback" present in the barrel is proportional to its distance from the body.

The modern cartridge was invented in France in 1835, and consists of a casing with a soft metal cap holding the primer charge. When struck by the gun's firing pin, the primer ignites the main propellant charge, expelling the bullet from the gun and leaving the case behind. This type of cartridge worked fine until the end of the nineteenth century and the invention of smokeless powder. Lead bullets just couldn't handle the new powder's increased propellant velocity. They were too soft to be gripped by the rifling and tended to get stripped, fouling the barrel. This led to the introduction of the metal-jacketed bullet, usually cupronickel (an alloy of copper and nickel).

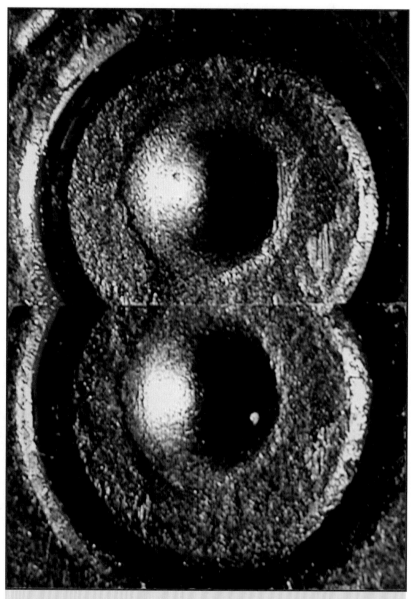

Here is a light micrograph comparison of two bullet casings, one retrieved from the scene of a shooting, the other taken from the gun of a suspect. A similar analysis was used to convict John Branion of the murder of his wife, Donna, in 1967. *Philippe Psaila/Photo Researchers, Inc.*

In 1912 Victor Balthazard, professor of forensic medicine at the Sorbonne in Paris, devised a means of matching bullets to firearms by use of photographs. Images were made of bullets fired from the suspected firearm, as well as the reference bullet. The photographs were then carefully enlarged, so that Balthazard could inspect the lands and grooves in microscopic detail. Balthazard applied these same photographic techniques to the examination and identification of cartridge casings using firing pin, breech face, ejector, and extractor marks.

Undoubtedly the greatest single advance in firearms examination came in the 1920s when Philip O. Gravelle, who together with Charles Waite founded the Bureau of Forensic Ballistics in New York, designed the comparison microscope. For the first time, the firearms examiner could study the reference bullet and the suspect bullet side by side and determine if they were fired by the same gun. If the width, depth, and spacing of a significant number of marks on both bullets are the same, an identification can be made.

Nowadays, the firearms examiner finds that assistance is often little more than a mouse click away. For several years a war raged between two competing software programs designed to automate the process of firearm and bullet identification. The FBI had DRUGFIRE, one of the first programs to link firearms evidence from different serial shooting investigations. Digital images of crime scene bullets, once fed into a computer, could be accessed instantly by any law enforcement agency that was hooked up to the system.

Over in the other camp, the Bureau of Alcohol, Tobacco, Firearms, and Explosives (ATF) championed IBIS (Integrated Ballistics Identification System). It worked along similar lines to DRUGFIRE. Photographs of the surface areas of a bullet and the primer/firing pin area of fired cartridge cases were stored in databases, along with such details as caliber, rifling specifications, date of crime, and date of entry. The program then listed possible matches, with the highest score at the top.

Frustratingly, DRUGFIRE and IBIS were incompatible, and software engineers began developing a unified program that all law enforcement agencies could access. The result was the National Integrated Ballistic Information Network. It is now used by more than 180 agencies, and since its inception in 1997 it has processed in excess of 1,286,500 pieces of crime scene evidence, and more than 20,300 "hits" have been logged, many of them yielding investigative information not obtainable by any other means.[4]

# Bloodstain Pattern Analysis:
## W. Thomas Zeigler Jr., 1975

Bodies are leaky objects: if punctured to any depth they tend to ooze or spray blood indiscriminately. This is hardly surprising, since the average-sized adult male has between five and six quarts of blood gurgling through their system (females and children have slightly less). Shooting, stabbing, or blunt-force trauma are the three main causes of crime scene bloodstain patterns. They can all produce astonishing quantities of blood. It can flow from a wound, it can drip, it can fly through the air.

Because blood is a uniform substance that responds well to the physics of fluid motion, the exit pattern it produces can often provide a revealing insight into just how the tragedy unfolded. It was the pioneering Austrian criminologist Hans Gross who first explored this possibility in the nineteenth century, but only in recent times has bloodstain pattern analysis entered the forensic mainstream. It is now a vital component of any crime investigation in which blood loss has occurred. The credit for much of this new-found importance must go to the American scientist Herbert Leon MacDonell, who received international acclaim for his work in the following case.

At 9:15 p.m. on Christmas Eve, 1975, the police in Winter Garden, a sleepy town in central Florida, received an emergency call: a prominent local businessman named Tommy Zeigler, age 30, had been shot and badly injured in an attempted robbery at his family's furniture store. When officers arrived at the store they found a bloodbath: four people shot and beaten to death. Only Tommy Zeigler was still alive, bleeding from a stomach wound. The dead included Zeigler's wife, Eunice, and her parents, Perry and Virginia Edwards. The other victim was a citrus worker named Charlie Mays, who, according to Zeigler, had been a member of the gang that raided the store.

Zeigler responded well to treatment—his injuries were less serious than originally feared—and he was able to give an account of the nightmarish events. Apparently, he and Ed Williams, a black part-time employee, had returned to the store at just after 7:00 p.m. to meet Charlie Mays, who had a TV set on layaway that he wanted to collect for Christmas. Zeigler said that once inside the store he was jumped by several attackers. In the melee he lost his spectacles, so he was unable to provide a good description of his assailants, other than that one was large and black. The brawl spilled over into Zeigler's office, where he had grabbed a pistol and had begun firing until he was hit by a bullet and collapsed.

Police Chief Don Ficke listened to this story thoughtfully. In recent weeks, two black criminals, dubbed the "Ski-Mask Bandits," had terrorized local businesses. Besides robbing their victims, the two thugs often sexually assaulted them as well. Ficke, aware that Mays's pants were undone, wondered if perhaps the dead man comprised one half of the notorious duo and Ed Williams the other. However, there was something else troubling the police chief: by chance a stray bullet had hit the store clock and stopped it at 7:24 p.m. Why, Ficke mused, if the shootings had taken place before half-past-seven, had Zeigler taken almost two hours to call for help?

The next day, Ed Williams went voluntarily to the police. He had heard rumors about the break-in and wanted to set the record straight. In Williams's version of events, Zeigler picked him up in his car, and then drove to the store. Zeigler went inside alone, calling out for Williams to follow. As Williams did so, Zeigler suddenly jumped out and shoved a gun into his chest. "For God's sake, Tommy, don't kill me," cried Williams.[1] Three times Zeigler pulled the trigger and three times the pistol jammed. This allowed the terrified Williams to flee for his life.

So who was lying? Suspicion veered sharply toward Zeigler when firearms experts reported that the bullets that killed Eunice and her parents came from a pair of .38s known to have been purchased by Tommy Zeigler. In total, 28 bullets were fired in the store that night, all from guns owned by Zeigler. Then came news that the Zeiglers had been having marital problems. Apparently Eunice had threatened to leave Tommy after Christmas. When it was learned that Tommy had recently insured Eunice's life for $500,000, the police decided to arrest him for murder.

But the district attorney's office needed to be cautious. Someone with Zeigler's hefty pocketbook could hire the very best in legal representation; only a watertight case would secure a conviction. To this end, they asked Herbert MacDonell, an industrial scientist who had turned the study and interpretation of bloodstains into a life's work, to examine the blood-drenched store. MacDonell's first view of the store came on January 7, 1976, and lasted all day. He spent hours on his hands and knees, measuring precisely, peering through a magnifying glass, and comparing stains with detailed crime-scene photographs. When he was through MacDonell was able to compile a chilling scenario.

Zeigler and his wife had entered the store through the rear door. Eunice went into the kitchen where she was shot in the back of her head. Her casual attitude—no sign of disarray and left hand still in her coat pocket—suggested to MacDonell that she had not seen any other bodies and was therefore the first person to be killed. A second bullet fired at Eunice had pierced the kitchen wall, stopping the clock on the other side of the wall, and timing the exact moment of her death at 7:24 p.m. MacDonell felt confident in saying this because the bullets, fired from the same weapon, had parallel trajectories.

Perry and Virginia Edwards were unintended victims. They had been en route to church, had probably noticed lights in the store, and had gone to investigate. Sheer misfortune landed them in the middle of a diabolical murder plot. A few paces inside the rear door, Perry Edwards was struck by a bullet. Dripping blood, he lurched toward the kitchen. Zeigler went after him with a linoleum crank. Edwards had reached Eunice—evidenced by his blood dripping onto her dead body—when Zeigler shot him again. Virginia Edwards,

## ⚲ THE FATHER OF CRIMINALISTICS

Although Hans Gross received very little formal academic training, he virtually invented what is today termed *criminalistics*.
At age 22 he left Graz University, where he had studied law, to
work as an examining magistrate, traveling the villages of his
homeland, Austria, listening to cases, passing sentences, and
assisting the police in investigating unsolved crimes. He was a
fastidious collector of details, both physical and psychological,
and for almost three decades used his courtroom as a kind of
social laboratory.

In 1893 he distilled all these observations into a book called
*System der Kriminalistik* (translated into English as *Criminal Investigation*). In this groundbreaking text Gross laid out the first truly
scientific system for tackling crime, employing such radical new
techniques as fingerprints, microscopy, and serology.

This book revolutionized crime detection and established Gross
as Europe's foremost criminologist. He trained judges and police
forces in his methods, and under his tutelage the Austrian police
became the most advanced in Europe. Earlier than anyone else he
saw the need for meticulous organization. This led him to assem-
ble his *untersucherkoffer*, a detective's briefcase with compart-
ments holding everything an investigator might need, including
rubber gloves, a measuring tape, scissors, test tubes, a magnifying
glass, and various fingerprint powders.

In 1902 he was honored with the chair in criminology at the
University of Prague. He was appointed professor of penal law
two years later at the university in his home city of Graz. Besides
his academic duties, he continued to assist the police on several
difficult cases. The culmination of his career came in 1912, at
Graz University, when he founded the world's first criminological
institute.

At age 67 he enlisted to fight in World War I and contracted a
fatal lung illness in the line of duty in 1915. By the time of his
death, *Criminal Investigation* had become the definitive reference
work of its kind, translated into several languages. It remains one
of the great books on forensic science.

cowering behind a sofa to escape her homicidal son-in-law, raised a protective hand as Zeigler loomed over her. A bullet grazed her finger before smashing into her skull.

Now Zeigler waited for Charlie Mays, unwittingly cast in the role of a Ski-Mask Bandit, to arrive. But the fates conspired once more against Zeigler—first the Edwardses, now Mays. The intended fall guy had company. Felton Thomas told investigators how he had gone with Mays to the store at 7:30 p.m. Zeigler had greeted them outside with a strange request: there was a bag full of guns on his car seat; would they mind test-firing the weapons for him at a nearby orange grove? Although mystified, both men agreed and climbed into Ziegler's car. Corroboration for this improbable-sounding diversion came when Thomas later led officers to the orange grove and pointed out fragments of .38 caliber shells. Afterward Zeigler drove at breakneck pace back to the store. Once there, he announced that he had forgotten his keys. If Charlie Mays wanted his TV for Christmas, he said, they would have to break in. Thomas declined and left. Mays stayed behind and entered the store with Zeigler.

Once inside, Mays was shot twice and then beaten to death with the linoleum crank. Although droplets of his blood fell onto that of Perry Edwards, the two had not mixed, an indication that Edwards had been dead for some time. A shoulder holster found near Mays's body, and meant to incriminate him, was an obvious plant. The kind of beating that killed Charlie Mays would have sprayed medium-velocity bloodstains over the holster's upper surface. There were none. The holster's back was also clean, even though the floor where it lay was drenched in blood. Clearly, the blood had dried—a process that MacDonell estimated would have taken at least 15 minutes—before the holster was dropped onto it.

But it was Zeigler's own blood that branded him a liar. He had been shot, he said, at the rear of the store, and from there he had struggled to the phone to summon help. Afterward he had waited at the front of the store. MacDonell tracked the drops of blood from the telephone to the storefront, but could find none elsewhere. Everything pointed to Zeigler having been standing by the phone when he was shot, and the only person who could have fired that shot was Zeigler himself.

On July 2, 1976, after a trial in which MacDonell's vivid reconstruction held the court spellbound, Zeigler was convicted of quadruple murder and later condemned to death.

In 1988 an appellate court decision overturned Zeigler's death sentence, and he was awarded a new sentencing hearing. The following year the original sentence was reimposed and Zeigler returned to death row, where he remains.

When reviewing a crime scene, the experienced bloodstain-pattern interpreter will seek the answers to seven questions:

1. The distance between the target surface and the origin of blood at the time of bloodshed
2. The point(s) of origin of the blood
3. Movement and direction of a person or an object
4. The number of blows, shots, etc., causing the bloodshed and/or the dispersal of blood
5. Type and direction of impact that produced the bloodshed
6. The position of the victim and/or object during bloodshed
7. Movement of the victim and/or object after bloodshed.

No matter how blood exits the body, it will always form some kind of pattern. This is largely dictated by the speed of impact and the distance of spatter travel, and is usually classified in three ways:

1. *Low velocity spatter*   Caused by an impact of less than five feet per second; blood cast off from fist, shoe, weapon, dripping, or splashing. The resulting blood spots are mostly 4 to 8 mm in diameter.
2. *Medium velocity spatter*   Caused by an impact of five to 25 feet per second; blows with a baseball bat, hammer, axe, or similar instrument. This produces blood spots typically about 4 mm in diameter.
3. *High velocity spatter*   Caused by an impact of 100 feet per second; almost always gunshot, but occasionally produced by contact with high velocity machinery. The smallest of all, these blood spots are typically less than 1 mm in diameter, producing a fine mist-like spray, much like an aerosol.

Another key factor in determining pattern type is surface texture. Blood hitting a hard, nonporous surface like a polished table tends to form smooth-edged stains. On an absorbent surface, like a carpet, the blood spots form jagged edges.

North Carolina State Bureau of Investigation agent Duane Deaver testifies during Michael Peterson's murder trial in August 2003. Deaver explained how his tests of blood spatters found inside the Peterson home strengthened his opinion that Michael's wife, Kathleen, was beaten to death. Bloodstain pattern evidence proved to be damning for Thomas Zeigler, who was found guilty of murdering his wife, Eunice, her parents, Perry and Virginia Edwards, and Charlie Mays. *AP/Sara Davis*

When an assailant uses either a knife or a blunt object to strike someone, the first blow will often cause an open wound, transferring blood to the weapon. As the attacker withdraws the weapon in preparing to strike again, blood will fly from its surface. Similarly, blood will be cast off the weapon as it is brought forward. In both instances, the cast-off blood spatter appears linear and the droplet size is generally quite small.

Gunshot wounds are equally illuminating. Here, there are two distinct patterns to look for. Forward spatter—the kind most often associated with exit wounds—is the product of blood traveling in the same direction as the bullet. Back spatter occurs when blood is blown back from an entrance wound by increased pressure from inside the tissues as the bullet impacts them. Often, with a firearm held in close proximity to the target, the inside of the barrel, as well as the gun itself, may sustain heavy back spatter.

Another factor is the impact angle made by the blood as it strikes a flat surface. A droplet falling vertically will create a much

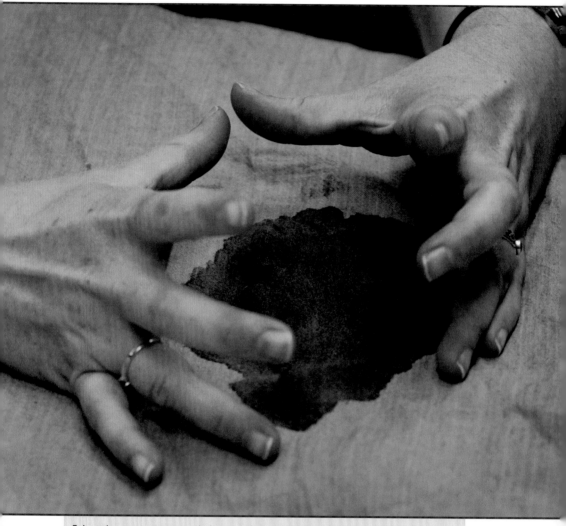

A teacher examines a stab wound and bloodstain on a piece of clothing from a mock crime scene while participating in a blood spatter analysis workshop during the Forensic Science Educational Conference in Indianapolis, Indiana, in June 2006. *AP/AJ Mast*

more circular stain than one that falls obliquely. As the oblique angle decreases, the more elongated the stain.

The shape of the individual drops in the overall pattern can reveal the direction from which the blood originated, as well as the trajectory of each drop. In the distinctive teardrop-shaped blood-stain, the pointed end of the stain faces the direction the stain is traveling. When a blood drop strikes a surface with considerable force and at an oblique angle, a smaller droplet, or satellite, is cast off from the larger drop, or parent, much like a breaking wave. This small cast-off blood travels close to the surface and, in a very short distance, begins to streak the surface. Usually, this stain appears as a very original, fine straight line with a round end marking the point at which the droplet's forward motion was terminated.

Arterial bleeding tends to create an entirely different staining pattern. Because the heart is still beating, pressure in the arteries forces blood to pulsate from an open wound, causing an indiscriminate spurting pattern rather than the flowing or dripping associated with other wounds.

When blood leaves the body, it may be transferred by direct contact to a weapon, another person, or an article of clothing. Transferred stains often appear as smears rather than distinct drops of blood. This can be very helpful in identifying the weapon used in an assault.

Even though bloodstain pattern analysis is as much art as science, it is firmly grounded in physics and the basic principles of geometry. Once all the answers to certain basic questions are in place, an experienced analyst can usually generate a three-dimensional model of the attack, often finding a key piece of information that may corroborate or contradict a suspect's story.

# Explosives:
## Steven Benson, 1985

A single bomb can cause more misery in a shorter time than any other lethal weapon. Scores, sometimes even hundreds, of people may have their lives extinguished at the press of a button or the flash of a fuse. Cheap to build, highly efficient, and virtually impossible to guard against, bombs have always been a favored weapon of terrorists. But political zealots cannot claim a monopoly; occasionally bombs are the tool of the everyday psychopath, someone motivated by nothing more sophisticated than greed.

Just before breakfast on July 9, 1985, Steven Benson, a 33-year-old electronics buff and heir to a tobacco fortune, was loading stakes and blueprints into a 1978 Chevrolet Suburban outside the family's palatial house in the Quail Creek subdivision of Naples, Florida. He and other family members had scheduled that day for marking out the lot for a new house. An hour or so later, at about 9:00 a.m., Steven accompanied his mother, Margaret Benson, 63; sister, Carol Lynn Kendall, 39; and adopted brother, Scott, 21, out to the Suburban. As they were about to drive off, Steven clucked his annoyance: he'd left a tape measure in the house. He tossed the keys to Scott and headed indoors. Seconds later Scott turned the key in the ignition and a massive orange flash enveloped the vehicle.

The Suburban just blew apart. Only Carol Lynn survived the blast, though with burns over 30 percent of her body. As she crawled away from the twisted shell, a second blast erupted, turning the Suburban into an inferno. And yet, when she looked up, she saw Steven running to the house. "I couldn't understand why he wasn't coming over to help me," she said later.[1]

The murder of such socially prominent citizens—the Bensons were very wealthy—sent shockwaves throughout Naples, and by 11:30 a.m. agents from the Bureau of Alcohol, Tobacco, Firearms, and Explosives were on the scene. Amid the twisted wreckage, scorched wire, and splinters from the wooden stakes, they found obvious signs of a crude bomb: fragments of galvanized pipe and two end caps. Steven Benson watched all this activity with obvious interest, seemingly unaffected by his brush with almost certain death.

When ATF explosives expert Albert Gleason began his examination of the shattered vehicle, he soon located the sources of the two explosions: one in the console area, the second beneath the rear passenger seat. This supported the conclusions of the Collier County Medical Examiner, Heinrich Schmid, who found that Margaret Benson's injuries were mostly on the left side of her body, and Scott's were on the right, strongly suggesting that at least one bomb had exploded between them.

A little-known quirk of explosives is just how much of the actual bomb is left intact after a blast. On this occasion Gleason established that the two bombs were each about a foot long, with four-inch end caps screwed on to pipes to seal the explosive. Two of the end caps were stamped with the manufacturer's mark, one with a letter *U* for *Union Brand*, another *G* for *Grinnell*, raising hopes that both seller and buyer might be traced. Pipe bombs are simple devices; their primary components are a canister (in this case a galvanized pipe threaded at both ends), an explosive device, and some kind of detonator. Gleason had already identified the bomb type, now he needed to know how it had been triggered.

He began by taping off a 25-foot perimeter around the blast core. Then, in a manner similar to archaeological excavators, he and other officers began sifting dirt through a wire strainer, then pawing at it with magnetized gloves. Before long they found the remains of four 1.5 D-cell batteries. Gleason reasoned that an electronically controlled switching device powered by 6 volts would detonate the bomb. Eventually, among the debris he found a small piece of a circuit board that did not appear to belong in the vehicle as well as a manual switch that couldn't be accounted for.

Elsewhere, other investigators were visiting local hardware stores, construction sites, plumbing supply shops, and junkyards, querying recent purchases of end caps and sections of galvanized

Steven Benson on trial for the bombing murder of his mother and adoptive brother in Miami in 1986. *Bettmann/Corbis*

pipe. One outlet, Hughes Building Supply in Naples, checked their records and found that they had sold two Union Brand end caps on July 5, and two foot-long sections of threaded pipe on July 8. The sales assistant described the customer as about six feet tall and 200 pounds, very similar to Steven Benson. He'd remembered the transaction vividly because it was for an unusually small amount.

Unfortunately, fingerprint analysis of the pipe bomb components came up blank. Then one of the investigators had a flash of inspiration: what about checking the two sales tickets at the supply store for prints? These were treated with chemicals. On the face of each was a latent palm print, what experts term a "writer's palm," made by someone left-handed, someone like Steven Benson.

After considerable legal wrangling, agents managed to obtain inked impressions of Benson's fingerprints, which matched those on the tickets.

In the meantime, the Benson family tree had revealed a sensational secret: it turned out that Scott Benson, whom everyone had thought was Steven's brother, was actually Carol Lynn's son, born out of wedlock when she was a teenager. To cover up the scandal Margaret Benson had adopted Scott and raised him as her son. From all accounts, she had doted on him, much to Steven's fury.

That wasn't Steven's only problem: he was also drowning in debt. A business venture had gone sour and he had been caught siphoning money from his mother's stock account. When Margaret Benson learned of her son's duplicity, she had threatened to disinherit him. It was this fear of financial ruin, agents speculated, that had driven Steven to eliminate his family, and thereby inherit the entire $10 million fortune. With his electronics expertise, the construction of a pipe bomb would be child's play. On August 21 Benson was arrested and 11 months later he stood trial for murder.

Although Carol Lynn remembered the blast had followed almost immediately after Scott turned the key, Gleason doubted that the ignition switch had triggered the explosions. He believed Benson had detonated the explosion by remote control. Although Gleason combed every inch of the crime scene, he was never able to locate the detonator itself, but those scraps of scorched circuit board and batteries convinced him that the blast had been detonated from outside the car.

To give some idea of just how powerful the bomb had been, Gleason showed the court what he believed to be a similar device. Empty, the length of pipe weighed 20 pounds, and could have held anywhere between three to six pounds of high explosives.

With the fingerprint evidence as well, it all made for a damning case. On August 8, 1986, Steven Benson was found guilty of first-degree murder and later sentenced to two life terms.

The criminal use of explosives falls into two categories: as an aid in furtherance of theft, such as attacking the locks of safes and strong-rooms (increasingly rare nowadays); and as a means of attacking persons or property, often in pursuit of some political agenda. Whatever the motivation, explosions remain among the most terrifying of modern experiences.

An explosion is produced by combustion accompanied by the creation of heat and gas. It is the sudden buildup of expanding gas pressure that causes the violent blast at the center of the explosion. Bombs can be classified as low explosive or high explosive, depending upon the speed of detonation (the chemical reaction time). The earliest known low explosive—black powder—is thought to have originated in China, where it was used in the tenth century A.D. for fireworks and signals. During the Middle

## ⚲ THE HISTORY OF CHROMATOGRAPHY

The most common technique for the analysis and identification of explosives is chromatography. Although nowadays a highly sophisticated laboratory tool, chromatography has its origins in much humbler surroundings. Early European dye makers were the first to adopt its principles. They found they could test their dye mixtures by dipping strings or pieces of cloth into a dye vat, and then watching closely as capillary action drew the solution up the inserted material. At various intervals bands of differing colors appeared on the material, and by studying these manufacturers could gauge the strength of their dyes.

Although various nineteenth-century chemists had attempted to adapt this principle to the laboratory, it was the Russian botanist Mikhail Tsvet who, beginning in 1906, established the basic principles that apply to this day.

Tsvet's technique was very simple. He packed a vertical glass column with an adsorptive material (one in which the molecules gather in a film on the surface), such as alumina, silica, cellulose, or charcoal. Then he added a solution of plant pigments to the top of the column and washed the pigments through the column with an organic solvent. As they passed through the column, the pigments separated into a series of colored bands on the column, divided by regions entirely free of pigments. Because Tsvet worked with colored substances, he called the method chromatography (from the Greek meaning "color writing").

Basically, all chromatography involves two phases: a mobile phase in which the substance is first dissolved in an appropriate solvent; and a stationary phase when the sample is passed

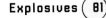

Ages black powder was supplanted by gunpowder, which is a mixture principally of potassium nitrate and charcoal together with some sulfur. The potassium nitrate is a very rich source of oxygen that combines with the carbon of the charcoal to form carbon dioxide.

If widely dispersed or loosely packed when detonated, low explosives, although still dangerous, lose much of their destructive power. It is the container that gives a low explosive its deadly dimension. A

through an adsorbent. As the elements in the sample migrate, their molecules attach themselves to the adsorbent. Because each compound has its own distinctive adsorption rate, this binding takes place at different times. By plotting these variances on a chart, then comparing that chart with a set of known reference values, the compound can be identified.

In gas chromatography—used for analyzing fire residue—a sample is vaporized and sent down a tube by an inert gas, where all the compounds in the sample separate. Because accelerants and explosive chemicals move down the tube at different rates than do other residue substances—usually ash, charred wood, plastic, or fiber—each compound settles in the tube at a different rate, called the retention time. By consulting a reference table of retention times, the compound may be ascertained.

For those compounds that would break down completely if vaporized, liquid chromatography, in which the sample is carried down the tube by a liquid, is used.

Another technique called thin-layer chromatography also uses a liquid to transport the sample. A glass slide is coated on one side with a thin layer of finely ground silica gel and spots of the sample are placed at the bottom of the slide. The slide is then partially immersed in a liquid, which, by capillary action, climbs up the slide and over the sample, separating its components. At this point the separations are generally colorless and must either be viewed under ultraviolet light or else sprayed with a suitable reagent that will colorize the result. The resulting chromatographic plate is then compared with other samples, or a control, for similarities.

simple pipe bomb can be constructed by emptying the black powder from a few shotgun shells into a pipe, closing the ends, and adding a fuse. When detonated, the compressed black powder produces a large volume of gas that expands violently, forcing the walls of the pipe to bulge and stretch and ultimately fragment, launching shrapnel in all directions. But it's the shockwave that does most of the damage, hurtling outward, as it does, at 3,000 feet per second.

High explosives, such as TNT (trinitrotoluene), dynamite, and PETN (pentaerythritol tetranitrate), are safer to transport and handle than low explosives, and for this reason are favored by the military and industry. In order to detonate, high explosive requires some kind of primer or blasting cap. The destructive power can be colossal, as high explosives explode almost instantaneously, with a shockwave expanding at a rate of up to 20,000 feet per second, shattering the intended target.

When investigating an explosion, experts will first define the area of debris fallout. This is critical. A commonly employed method is to estimate the distance from the center of the explosion to the furthest piece of debris, then seal off an area with a radius 50 percent greater than this. Everything within this zone should be investigated thoroughly.

Dents, holes, and scars in vertical surfaces can help pinpoint the center of the explosion. From there, visual inspection of the damage normally indicates the direction of the shockwave. Long metal objects, such as piping, railings, and window frames—even long nails, screws, or bolts—bend away from the direction of the blast. Metal surfaces on items like refrigerators or washing machines show a "dishing" effect, as do other empty metal containers. If, however, a metal container is full—a water tank or radiator, for instance—it will retain its shape, because the liquids inside are virtually incompressible. By subjecting similar objects to laboratory tests, it is usually possible to determine the amount of pressure that caused the damage, and, from this, the nature and quantity of the explosive can be estimated.

Embedded fragments help determine whether the explosive was in some kind of container, and, if so, what form that container took. Pieces of the detonator, such as wires and the crimping cap, mechanical detonating devices, or small fragments of a timing device, may also be found. Laboratories that specialize in explosives analysis maintain a comprehensive collection of commercial

Officials [*right*] survey the damage to a broadcast tower caused by the bomb that detonated among Olympic revelers in Atlanta's Centennial Olympic Park during the 1996 Summer Games. *Dimitri Iundt/ TempSport/Corbis*

products, from which it is often possible to identify the manufacturer and source of the explosive and its detonator.

The blast from an explosion is notoriously unpredictable. Ordinarily, structural elements tend to be blown outward, as do most movable objects. But anomalies do occur. For instance, when the area of low pressure that follows the shock wave passes over horizontal surfaces, such as kitchen worktops, it will often suck them upward. To the untrained eye, this might give the erroneous impression that the original explosion took place beneath them.

Nowadays explosives are rarely seen in burglaries. The modern thief prefers thermic lances or a plasma cutting torch to gain access to a troublesome safe. It is in the world of terrorism where explosives have assumed their most lethal incarnation.

Bombs can slaughter thousands and profoundly affect the lives of millions more. Whether homegrown or international, the determined terrorist has easy access to a frightening array of explosive devices. The fertilizer-based bomb that caused such mayhem in Oklahoma in 1995 was similar in construction to the device used in the World Trade Center bombing two years earlier. On that occasion the twin towers withstood the assault, but as the ghastly events of September 11, 2001, demonstrate, the suicide bomber doesn't even have to construct his own device; others do it for him. Twenty thousand gallons of high-octane jet fuel encased in pressured containers, traveling at 500 miles per hour, needs only the intervention of a deranged hand to convert it into the deadliest criminal use of explosives yet seen.

# DNA:
# Colin Pitchfork, 1987

Even though the discovery of chemical DNA can be dated to 1863, it was the Russian-born biochemist Phoebus Levene, in 1911, who discovered that individual cells contain a nucleus made up of nucleic acid. After Levene, another three decades would pass before DNA's role in genetic inheritance was demonstrated. In 1943 the American bacteriologist Oswald Avery proved that DNA is the substance that dictates not only our hair and eye color, but also everything else about our physical appearance. From here hopes grew that DNA analysis might one day figure in the crime-fighting spectrum. That day came to pass in England in 1987.

It was 7:20 a.m. on November 22, 1983, when a hospital porter making his way to work in the village of Narborough, near Leicester, took his usual shortcut along a lonely footpath known as The Black Pad. A few yards along the lane he saw, sprawled on some grass, the body of 15-year-old Lynda Mann. She had been strangled. Trace evidence showed that the killer was blood group A and a secretor (one of the 80 percent of the population who secrete their blood type in other bodily fluids, such as saliva), with a strong phosphoglucomutase (PGM) 1+ enzyme. Taken together, these factors occur in only 10 percent of the adult male population, a scarcity that heartened detectives. It might not be able to positively identify the killer, but it would certainly slash the number of possible suspects.

Initial inquiries centered on Carlton Hayes Hospital, a nearby mental institution. When that proved fruitless the search expanded to include the nearby villages of Enderby and Littlethorpe. Although convinced that the killer was a local man, investigators canvassing the tri-village area were stymied at every turn. Only later would the awful realization sink in that they actually questioned the killer during this sweep. The computer had flagged the man for two reasons:

1. He had previous convictions for sexual offenses.
2. He had been referred to Carlton Hayes Hospital for therapy as an outpatient.

When interviewed, the man was unable to provide an alibi for the time of the murder. He claimed to have been babysitting his son. Despite this, the fact that he had lived a few miles outside what police regarded as the probable catchment area outweighed all other considerations, and he was eliminated from the inquiry. (He did not move to Littlethorpe until a month after the killing of Lynda Mann.) Also, the likelihood of a parent taking time off from babysitting duties to commit such an atrocious murder was thought too grotesque to consider.

Hampered by a lack of clues, the murder investigation gradually ran out of steam. On the first anniversary of Lynda's death someone left a tiny cross at the spot where her body was found. A year later the commemorative ritual was repeated. Before it could happen a third time the killer struck again.

Dawn Ashworth was also 15 years old. A schoolgirl from Enderby, she went missing on July 31, 1986. Two days later her body was found less than a mile from the spot where Lynda Mann met her death. Dawn had been savagely attacked and tests confirmed that detectives were hunting a dual-killer. Almost immediately investigators got a break; a teenage kitchen porter at Carlton Hayes Hospital came forward and confessed to this latest killing. Even though a blood test showed he was not a PGM 1+, A secretor, his confession had the ring of authenticity to it, especially to those officers who had spent almost three years tracking Lynda Mann's killer, and despite the youth's insistence that he knew nothing about the first murder.

One person convinced that the youth was a fantasist, uninvolved in either killing, was the suspect's father. A thought occurred to him. Recently, the local papers had carried accounts of a young scientist and something called genetic fingerprinting. He wondered: could this help his son?

Professor Alec Jeffreys, who discovered DNA fingerprinting, holds a copy of the first DNA fingerprint profile in this September 2004 photo. *AP/Rui Vieira/PA*

It was in the fall of 1984 that Dr. Alec Jeffreys, a research fellow at Leicester University's Lister Institute, stumbled upon the discovery that would revolutionize crime fighting around the globe. Even though DNA had been studied for decades, it was Jeffreys who perfected the means whereby identifiable genetic markers could be developed on an X-ray film as a kind of bar code and then compared with other specimens. Jeffreys was asked to extract DNA left by the killer and compare it to the kitchen porter's blood sample. His results stunned those leading the investigation: not only had the porter not killed Lynda Mann, but he hadn't killed Dawn Ashworth, either! His entire confession had been a fabrication. Just about the only consolation that Jeffreys could offer the jaded officers was confirmation that one man had killed both girls. On November 21, 1986, legal and forensic history was made when the kitchen porter became the first person to be acquitted through DNA typing.

For those detectives charged with tracking down the double-killer the verdict had wider ramifications: If DNA typing was so accurate, why not conduct a mass testing of the local male population?

Early in 1987 the decision was made to draw blood from every local male between 16 and 34 years of age for DNA testing. By the end of January 1,000 men had been tested, but only a quarter cleared. This was due to the laboratories being overwhelmed by samples. In its original form DNA typing was a time-consuming procedure, often taking weeks. The process has now been reduced to a matter of days, but it is still much slower than fingerprinting, which can provide almost instant results.

It was the same the following month: hundreds more tests, still no identification. While the police doubted that the killer would volunteer blood, they were hoping to flush him out. Anyone who refused to cooperate soon found himself subjected to intense scrutiny. It was a war of nerves that paid off.

On August 1, 1987, a quartet of drinkers in a Leicester pub, all bakery workers, were discussing the notorious sexual liaisons of a fellow employee named Colin Pitchfork, when one of the four, Ian Kelly, dropped a conversational thunderbolt. Pitchfork, he said, had bullied him into taking the blood test on his behalf. A deathly hush fell over the table. It was broken at last by the other man present, who said that Pitchfork had approached him also, offering £200

($300) if he would act as a stand-in, but he had declined. Pitchfork had told both men that he was scared to take the test because his record—he had convictions for indecent exposure—meant that the police would give him a hard time. Kelly, a timid, malleable person, finally caved in under Pitchfork's relentless pressure and, using a faked passport, had gone along and given blood in Pitchfork's name.

A woman sitting at the table listened to these revelations with an anxiety born of suspicion. Like everyone who worked at the bakery, she knew Pitchfork as an overbearing lecher, forever harassing the female employees. But did that make him a murderer? For six weeks she wrestled with her conscience, then contacted the police.

First, detectives arrested Kelly; later that day, September 19, 1987, they called at the Littlethorpe home of 27-year-old Colin Pitchfork. He took his arrest philosophically and made no attempt to deny either killing. A sample of his blood was rushed to Jeffreys's laboratory for analysis. The genetic bar code was identical to that of the DNA sample from the killer-rapist. Colin Pitchfork was the 4,583rd male to be tested, and the last. The principle of DNA typing had been vindicated.

On January 22, 1988, Pitchfork pleaded guilty to both murders and was imprisoned for life.

Before the advent of DNA, the analysis of bodily fluids relied on more basic tools. Foremost among these was the ABO blood grouping system discovered by Karl Landsteiner in 1901. From this, other blood-related indicators such as the Rh factor (whether or not the sample contains the rhesus protein) or PGM (see above) were developed. All were highly useful but none was conclusive. They served more to exclude suspects than to identify the perpetrator. DNA changed all that. At last, investigators had a tool that could point the finger definitively at one person.

So how does DNA work? The answer lies in the four chemicals that make up DNA: adenine, guanine, cytosine, and thymine. These combine in a pattern that resembles a long, spiraling ladder. Around 99 percent of our genes are identical because each of us has the same body parts and organs; it is the remaining 1 percent that makes us unique. This is the segment of DNA that scientists analyze to identify an individual.

## 🔎 DEATH ROW AND DNA

As the Pitchfork case demonstrated, DNA profiling doesn't just convict the guilty, it can also free those wrongfully imprisoned. One of the most egregious examples of a false conviction came in 1985 when a Baltimore fisherman, Kirk Bloodsworth, was sentenced to death for the 1984 murder of nine-year-old Dawn Hamilton. At his trial no fewer than five eyewitnesses placed Bloodsworth with the victim.

On appeal, Bloodsworth was granted a retrial. He was again found guilty and this time given two life sentences. In 1992 his defense team received permission to retest crime scene trace evidence using the new technique of DNA typing. Two laboratories, including the FBI, eliminated Bloodsworth as the source of the samples recovered from the crime scene. On June 28, 1993, after nine years behind bars, Bloodsworth walked free, the first American to have a murder conviction overturned by DNA profiling.

Any lingering doubts about Bloodsworth's guilt were banished years later when the DNA sample led authorities to a convict already serving 45 years for attempted murder. On May 20, 2004, Kimberly Ruffner pleaded guilty to Dawn's murder and was sentenced to life imprisonment. In the bitterest of ironies, while incarcerated, Bloodsworth, who worked as the prison librarian, often took books to Ruffner's cell.

According to the Innocence Project, an organization dedicated to overturning wrongful convictions, since 1993 no fewer than 16 death row inmates in the United States have been exonerated through the use of DNA profiling.[1]

The procedure for creating a DNA fingerprint can best be shown in the following steps (the sample used is blood, but it could be any bodily fluid or item of human tissue):

1. Blood samples are collected from the victim, defendant, and crime scene.
2. White blood cells are separated from red blood cells.
3. DNA is extracted from the nuclei of white blood cells.
4. A restrictive enzyme is used to cut fragments of the DNA strand.

5. DNA fragments are put into a bed of gel with electrodes at either end.
6. Electric current sorts DNA fragments by length.
7. An absorbent blotter soaks up the imprint; it is radioactively treated, and an X-ray photograph (called an autoradiograph) is produced.

Once the autoradiograph has been analyzed and a match found, it is then a question of probabilities: what is the statistical likelihood of two people sharing this DNA profile? The answer, frequently, is billions to one.

If only a small amount of DNA is available for fingerprinting, a polymerase chain reaction (PCR) may be used to create thousands of copies of a DNA segment quickly and accurately. Developed in 1983 by the Nobel Prize-winning American biochemist Kary B. Mullis, PCR allows the investigator to obtain the large quantities of DNA necessary for high-quality analysis. It is a three-step process

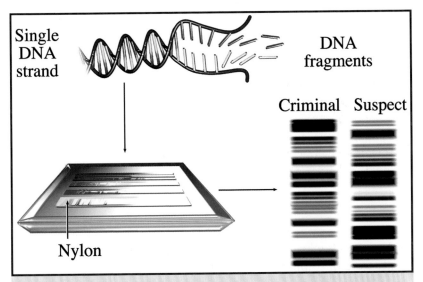

In this illustration a sample of nylon clothing is tested to see if DNA fragments are present. Once found, the DNA is tested using gel electrophoresis in order to compare the DNA of the criminal and the suspect. A similar process was vital in the conviction of Colin Pitchfork for the murder of Lynda Mann and Dawn Ashworth. *Visuals Unlimited/Corbis*

carried out in repeated cycles and requires as little as a single DNA molecule to serve as a template.

The initial step—denaturation or separation of the two strands of the DNA molecule—is achieved by heating the sample to around 95°C (203°F). Each strand is a template on which a new strand is built. Steps two and three involve cooling and reheating the sample, a process that doubles the number of copies. At the end of the cycle, which lasts about five minutes, the process begins again. Usually 25 to 30 cycles produce a sufficient amount of DNA to test. The technique has been used to amplify DNA fragments found in preserved tissues, such as those of a 40,000-year-old frozen woolly mammoth or of a 7,500-year-old human found in a peat bog.

Another, even more sophisticated innovation, is a still controversial technique known as low copy number (LCN) DNA analysis. In the past, conventional DNA testing required approximately 150 cells of genetic material for testing. However, crime scene investigators were frequently harvesting samples of less than that amount. In evidentiary terms, they were worthless. Then, in 1999, British scientists pioneered a method of micro-analysis whereby they could obtain a DNA profile from as few as 30 cells. By 2007, scientists had lowered the threshold to an astonishing *six cells'* worth of genetic material! Sensitivity of this order allows them to test even the skin cells left on a smudged fingerprint.

LCN analysis works by amplifying—or copying—the DNA in cycles, as in conventional testing. The difference lies in the numbers. Conventional testing generally calls for 28 cycles; LCN testing requires at least 32 cycles. Unfortunately, with each cycle, the DNA loses clarity. Think of it as a photocopy of a photocopy; the first copy might be acceptable but with each repetition the image degrades.

This isn't the only problem with LCN analysis. Contamination is an ever-present danger. Say, for example, a person shakes hands with someone who then goes on to commit a crime; it is possible that an innocent person's DNA might be transferred to the crime scene. If it has been, chances are that LCN analysis will find it and that person could have the police knocking on his or her door. Taken in isolation, this alone would be cause for grave concern, but there is another serious downside to LCN analysis: the testing procedure actually destroys the sample. This poses enormous problems in the courtroom. A prosecutor might well claim that LCN analysis has placed the defendant at a crime scene, but if the defense is unable to physically examine the sample themselves, then they have no means of rebutting that allegation. Such an uneven playing field has led many countries to declare a judicial moratorium on LCN testimony until more research is carried out.

Concerns such as these have tarnished DNA's reputation in recent years and have placed an increased burden on the crime scene investigators actually harvesting the evidence. Nothing less than the most scrupulous attention to detail will suffice. Despite this, DNA profiling continues to prosper and with good reason. It is nothing less than the greatest advance in forensic science since the advent of fingerprinting. DNA's importance has led the federal government to establish the Combined DNA Index System, or CODIS. This is a software program that consolidates state and national databases of DNA profiles from convicted offenders into a single searchable database.

# Time Since Death:
## Albert Walker, 1996

Whenever a body is discovered in suspicious circumstances, three vital questions are asked: Who is it? How did that person die? How long have they been dead? It is the answer to that last question that has caused some of the biggest controversies in the history of criminology. For despite what some detective novels and TV shows depict, there are few things more difficult than discerning exactly when a human being ceased to live. Most of the clues to this conundrum are organic, arising from observation of changes in the body itself, but occasionally the answer is derived from somewhere entirely unexpected.

On July 28, 1996, a commercial fishing boat trawling the south coast of Devon, England, hauled in its nets and made a gruesome discovery. Among that day's catch was a male dead body. A deep cut to the back of the head, and another gouge on his upper left hip were the only injuries, though neither wound was thought suspicious. Both injuries could have resulted from the body either striking a rock or being hit by a boat propeller. Also in the net, though not attached to the body, was an anchor. At autopsy the pathologist estimated that the body had been in the water for about seven days. There was nothing about the body to aid identification—except a Rolex wristwatch.

It was the Rolex that unlocked the key to the man's identity. Factory records logged the serial number to a Ronald Joseph Platt, who was traced to a rental address in Chelmsford, Essex. The landlords were unable to help with Platt's current whereabouts, however they did direct police to one of the missing man's friends, David Davis.

Davis lived in nearby Woodham Walter, but when a detective called at Davis's farmhouse, he knocked at the wrong house, only to be told that he must be mistaken—nobody named Davis lived next door, but there was an American called Platt. Puzzled, detectives did some background checks and soon uncovered a startling fact: for the past three years, Davis had been living every aspect of his life as Ronald Platt.

When officers did gain access to the nondescript farmhouse, they just stood and gaped. It was like Aladdin's Cave—stuffed with gold bars, oil paintings, and a huge selection of false identity documents.

David Davis wriggled and twisted, but slowly his façade crumbled. His real name was Albert Walker, and he was not American; he was a 50-year-old Canadian. In 1990 he had fled Ontario to escape 37 charges of theft, fraud, and money laundering involving millions of dollars. By the time of his arrest, he had risen to number four on Interpol's most-wanted list.

Walker had arrived in Britain with his daughter Sheena, then age 15, in December 1990. Courtesy of countless false identities, he continued to launder his stolen millions through a bewildering maze of accounts, and then, in late 1991, he met Ronald Platt, a gullible dupe with dreams of living in Canada. When Walker offered to finance his ambition, Platt jumped at the opportunity and took off for Canada, blissfully unaware that as soon as he left, Walker assumed his identity.

Living as Ron and Noelle Platt, husband and wife, Walker and his daughter had not attracted suspicion. Indeed, they prospered, and might have continued to do so, had not Platt returned, penniless, to England in 1995. Police suspected that with this unexpected reappearance Platt unwittingly signed his death warrant. Walker, now well established as a financial adviser, was prepared to pay any price to preserve his new identity, even if that meant killing Ronald Platt.

But was there any evidence to say that Platt had actually been murdered?

Suddenly a member of the investigative team remembered that gouge on Platt's hip, and he also recalled the anchor. What if Platt had been rendered unconscious and then that anchor had been hooked over his belt before he was thrown in the water? Could a chafing anchor have caused that hip injury? A pathologist conceded the possibility and a full-scale search for the anchor began. Because the anchor had been unattached to the body, the trawlermen had thought the two items unconnected, and therefore sold the anchor at a flea market. In November 1996, after three months of laborious searching, police finally managed to track down the missing anchor. Sure enough, when samples from belt and anchor were analyzed, both were found to contain similar traces of speckled zinc.

The investigation now gathered steam. It was learned that on July 8, 1996—three weeks before the body was found—someone had gone into a marine supply shop in Devon with a credit card in the name of R. J. Platt and purchased an identical anchor to the one used to weigh down the body. This credit card was found in Walker's possession when he was arrested.

On Walker's boat, *The Lady Jane,* investigators found a bag with the dead man's fingerprints on it and a cushion that held samples of what looked like Platt's hair. Walker silkily admitted that he and Platt had gone sailing on July 7, and that a large wave had caught the boat awkwardly, sending Platt sprawling and banging his head. But they had returned safely to shore and Platt had departed. He said he had not seen him again. Walker's story seemed unbreakable, as did his insistence that he had never been near the spot where Platt's body was found, until searchers visited a storage unit that Walker had rented. Hidden inside was a GPS navigational system.

The global positioning satellite system has revolutionized navigation on sea and land. At its heart is a network of orbiting satellites whose locations are continuously monitored by stations around the globe. The satellite transmits a radio signal at a steady frequency. A stationary observer detects a higher frequency as the satellite approaches and a lower one as it recedes. Measuring the speed of this frequency drop determines the distance of the observer from the satellite's track.

At the instant of the satellite's closest approach, the observed frequency is the same as that transmitted, so at that time the observer must be located somewhere along the line at right angles to the satellite's track. Since this orbit over the earth's surface is accurately known at all times, this reading, combined with the distance measurement, pinpoints the observer's position.

Walker's GPS system proved to be his undoing. A computer download showed the final coordinates of where that handset had been turned off. These plotted the position of the *Lady Jane* to about three miles off the south Devon coast—right where the body was found—at 8:59 p.m. on July 20, 1996.

Tidal flow experts confirmed that a 10-pound anchor was more than sufficient to take Platt's body to the bottom. Then came a string of experiments to see if currents in the crime scene area were sufficient to move such a weighted body. They concluded that Platt had been dumped where he was found.

Then there was the Rolex. It was, from all accounts, Platt's pride and joy. When recovered from the sea the watch showed 11:35 a.m. on July 22. If it had been fully wound—and Platt was known to be a stickler about this—it would have continued to operate for between 40 and 45 hours. Tracking back from the stopped watch suggested that Platt had been thrown overboard at some time between 2:35 p.m. and 7:35 p.m. on July 20, just an hour or so from when the GPS log placed Walker's boat at the crime scene.

All this information was gleaned from a single watch. It not only identified the victim, it also provided strong circumstantial evidence to the time that he died. If Walker had ditched the Rolex, he would have gotten away with murder. As it was, on July 6, 1998, he was jailed for life.

Nothing in forensic science is trickier—or has caused more bitter disputes—than the problem of establishing the time of death in murder victims. It is a fiendishly difficult business, made harder still with each passing hour that the body remains unfound, until a point is reached where associated or environmental evidence, rather than anatomical changes, is likely to furnish more reliable data. Here, though, we shall confine ourselves to anatomical changes.

Traditionally, three indicators are used to determine how long a person has been dead: rigor mortis, hypostasis (livor mortis), and body temperature (algor mortis). A fourth indicator, putrefaction, is factored in when dealing with bodies found some considerable time after death. None is wholly reliable, and, as we shall see, all are subject to huge variations.

Rigor mortis is a stiffness of the body caused by muscles contracting after death as glycogen is converted into lactic acid. It usually begins to show three hours after death in the muscles of the face and eyelids, and then spreads slowly through the body to the

## ⚲ TAKING A BITE OUT OF CRIME

It was forensic odontology—the study of teeth—that conclusively identified Ronald Platt. Teeth are an excellent source of information. This is because, of all the components of the human body, virtually nothing outlasts the teeth after death.

It is frequently claimed that no two people have identical teeth; however, it should be remembered that, unlike fingerprints, which remain unchanged from birth, teeth achieve their uniqueness through use and wear. For successful identification, both ante- and post-mortem records must be available. From such data, it is often possible to make an identification from a single tooth.

There are an estimated 200 different tooth-charting methods in use throughout the world. All provide a means of identification that is almost 100 percent reliable. The American approach, called the Universal System, allocates a different number to each of the 32 adult teeth, beginning with the upper right third molar (1), round the mouth to the lower right third molar (32). Information is recorded about the five visible surfaces of each tooth, from which it is generally possible to complete a dental grid, or odontogram, unique to that individual.

This individuality has given rise to another branch of odontology, bite-mark analysis, and here the forensic examiner is on far shakier ground. Many killers bite their victims, leaving ugly marks on the body, and often the perpetrator has been identified by the evidence of their own teeth. In recent years, however, a cluster of miscarriages of justice have cast doubts on the value of bite-mark analysis.

One of the worst examples began in 1992 when a Syracuse, New York, resident named Roy Brown was convicted for murder after a local dentist testified that it was Brown's teeth that made bite marks found on the victim's body. After years of petitions and motions, permission was finally given for the victim's corpse to be exhumed. Swab traces taken from the bite-mark revealed another man's DNA. (The prime suspect had already committed suicide in 2004 by stepping in front of a train after Brown had written him a letter.) In 2007 Brown was freed after serving 15 years for a murder that he did not commit. His ordeal led one of America's foremost odontologists, Dr. Richard Souviron, to state: "If you say that this bite fits this person and nobody else in the world, and if you use the bite-mark as the only piece of physical evidence linking an attacker to his victim, that's not science—that's junk."[1]

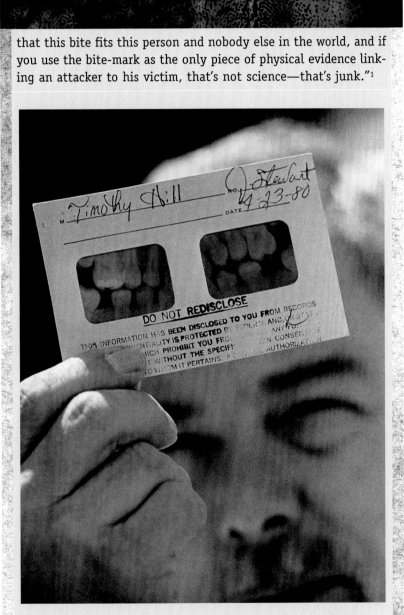

This March 31, 1981, photo shows a medical examiner displaying a set of dental x-rays used to help identify the body of a child, Timothy Hill, who had been missing since March 13. *AP/Joe Holloway, Jr.*

arms and legs, taking about 12 hours to complete. In the majority of cases the process begins to reverse after approximately 36 hours, until the body is soft and supple again. However, temperature and climate affect this. Heat accelerates the process and cold slows it down. In extremely hot climates, the onset of putrefaction may completely displace rigor within 9 to 12 hours of death.

Prolonged muscular activity shortly before death—such as exhaustion caused by fighting for one's life or convulsions—will not only hasten the onset of rigor, but also shorten its duration. Conversely, a late onset of rigor in many sudden deaths is sometimes explained by a lack of muscular activity immediately prior to death. So many variables have led some medical examiners to entirely discount rigor mortis as a means of estimating the time of death; for others it remains an invaluable, if highly contentious, tool.

Hypostasis is a dark discoloration of the skin resulting from the gravitational pooling of blood in the lower parts of the body when circulation ceases. The process begins immediately after the circulation stops and is present in all bodies, although it may be inconspicuous in some and thus escape notice. Hypostasis also develops in a time sequence and is first apparent about 30 minutes after death. As the red cells break down, evacuate the capillaries, and enter the body, dull red patches or blotches appear on the lower skin levels. These patches deepen in intensity and combine over the succeeding hours to form extensive areas of reddish-purple discoloration, a process that generally takes from six to 10 hours. The color then becomes fixed. If a person dies in bed lying on his back, the discoloration would normally be found on his back. Any lividity found on the front part of the body would indicate some postmortem movement.

Body temperature (algor mortis) is the third and probably the most useful indicator of time of death, especially if the victim has been dead for less than 24 hours. After death, when oxygen is no longer fueling the body and keeping it warm, the body temperature falls until it reaches the temperature of its surroundings. Musculature and ambient temperature play significant roles. An obese person will cool much more slowly than a lean person; children lose heat more quickly than adults; someone who dies in a warm room will retain more body heat than someone who succumbs outdoors in cold weather. On balance, algor mortis is more reliable

John Butts, chief medical examiner for University of North Carolina Hospitals in Chapel Hill, poses in his lab in this February 2004 photo. The work done in his lab and those like it often answers key questions in murder investigations, including the victim's time of death. AP/Sara D. Davis

in temperate or cool climates. Tropical climates may cause only a minimal fall in body temperature, while in exceptionally hot countries the temperature may even rise after death.

Various formulas have been devised in an attempt to provide a mathematical means of calculating time of death. The following is fairly typical:

$$\frac{\text{Normal temp (98.6°F) - Rectal temp}}{1.5} = \text{Approx. hours since death}$$

In recent times, medical examiners have tended to shy away from the mathematical model because of the bewildering number of variables. These, then, are the conventional means of establishing time of death, but there are others.

Putrefaction is the post-mortem destruction of bodily soft tissues caused by the action of bacteria and enzymes. Environmental temperature has an enormous effect on putrefaction. In a temperate climate, the degree of putrefaction reached after 24 hours at the height of summer may take as long as two weeks in the depth of winter. High humidity also speeds up putrefaction.

Other factors useful in estimating the time of death—such as stomach contents, insect infestation, and forensic anthropology— fall outside the scope of this book, but all are useful. Again, though, it cannot be emphasized strongly enough that none of the above tests is 100 percent accurate. Only by factoring in all the results can a likely time of death be achieved.

# Chronology

| | |
|---|---|
| **Third century B.C.** | Alexandrian physicians Erasistratus and Herophilus conduct the first autopsies. |
| **44 B.C.** | Antistius performs an autopsy on Julius Caesar. |
| **1194** | Office of Coroner is originated in England, first referred to as *custos placitorum* ("keeper of the pleas") in the Articles of Eyre. The name was originally "crowner," or "coronator," derived from corona, meaning "crown." |
| **1248** | A Chinese book, *Hsi Duan Yu* (the Washing Away of Wrongs), contains rudimentary descriptions of how to distinguish suspicious deaths. This was the first recorded application of medical knowledge to the solution of crime. |
| **1447** | Missing teeth are used to identify the body of the Duke of Burgundy in France. |
| **1507** | The first European book to acknowledge the usefulness of physicians in legal cases, *Constitutio Bambergenis Criminalis* (Criminal Code for the German city of Bamberg), is published in Bavaria. |
| **1663** | Danish physician Thomas Bartholin devises a test to establish if a dead baby had been stillborn or the victim of infanticide. Air in the lungs would be proof that the baby had breathed. |
| **1670** | The first simple microscope with powerful lenses is created by Anton Van Leeuwenhoek of Holland. |
| **1775** | The body of U.S. General Joseph Warren is identified by engraver Paul Revere, who had made his false teeth. |
| **1813** | Mathieu Orfila publishes *Traite des Poisons ou Toxicologie General* (The Effects of Poisons, or General Toxicology). |
| **1817** | Francois-Eugène Vidocq forms the first police detective bureau in Paris, forerunner of la Sûreté. |

**1823** The first paper to discuss the nature of fingerprints is published by John Evangelista Purkinje, a professor of anatomy at the University of Breslau, Czecheslovakia.

**1829** Scotland Yard is formed.

**1835** Henry Goddard, Scotland Yard detective, begins to make comparisons between bullet striations and the rifling in gun barrels.

**1836** James Marsh develops his "mirror" test for arsenic.

**1851** Belgian chemist Jean Servais Stas becomes the first to identify vegetable poisons in body tissue.

**1858** Sir William Herschel requires natives in Hooghly district in India to affix fingerprints to contracts as a means of identification.

**1859** Spectroscopy is developed. Gustav Kirchoff and Robert Bunson showed that substances give off a spectrum of light that identifies elements in the substance.

**1865** Alfred Swaine Taylor publishes *The Principles and Practice of Medical Jurisprudence.*

**1879** A system of identifying people by taking several body measurements (anthropometry) is developed by Alphonse Bertillon.

**1880** Henry Faulds publishes a paper in the journal *Nature,* suggesting that fingerprints at the scene of a crime could identify the offender.

**1884** Chicago creates the first municipal Criminal Identification Bureau.

**1888** Alphonse Bertillon develops full-face and profile photographs as mug shots, and the *portrait parle* (speaking likeness) of suspects.

**1892** The first murderer, Francesca Rojas in Argentina, is convicted through the use of fingerprint evidence.

Sir Francis Galton publishes *Finger Prints,* the first comprehensive book on the nature of fingerprints and their use in solving crime.

**1893** Hans Gross publishes his seminal work, *System der Kriminalistik (Criminal Investigation).*

**1897** The National Bureau of Criminal Identification is established by the International Association of Chiefs of Police (IACP) and located in Chicago.

**1900–1901** Paul Uhlenhuth develops the precipitin test to distinguish human blood from animal blood

**1901** Karl Landsteiner discovers human blood groups.

Sir Edward Henry, Commissioner at Scotland Yard, advocates the adoption of fingerprint identification to replace anthropometry.

**1902** A burglar, Harry Jackson, becomes the first British person convicted using fingerprint evidence.

**1903** The New York State Prison system begins the first systematic use of fingerprints in the United States for criminal identification.

**1905** The Bureau of Investigation (later the Federal Bureau of Investigation, or FBI) is established.

**1910** Edmond Locard establishes the world's first forensic laboratory in Lyon, France.

American handwriting expert Albert S. Osborn's pioneering *Questioned Documents* leads to the acceptance of such testimony in court.

**1915** The first antibody test for ABO blood groups is developed by Leone Lattes in Italy.

The International Association for Criminal Identification (to become The International Association of Identification) is organized in Oakland, California.

**1918** In New York City the Chief Medical Examiner's Office is founded.

**1921** John Larson and Leonard Keeler design the polygraph.

**1923** Calvin H. Goddard refines Phillip O. Gravelle's comparison microscope for use in ballistics examinations.

**1925** The Bureau of Forensic Ballistics is founded in New York City by Goddard, Gravelle, Charles E. Waite, and John H. Fisher.

**1930** The National fingerprint file is set up in the United States by the Bureau of Investigation.

**1932** The Bureau of Investigation crime laboratory is established.

**1935** The Bureau of Investigation is renamed the Federal Bureau of Investigation (FBI).

**1941** Voice spectrography study begins at Bell Labs.

**1945** Frank Lundquist, working at the Legal Medicine Unit at the University of Copenhagen, develops the acid phosphatase test for semen.

**1952** A.T. James and A.J.P. Martin invent the gas chromatograph.

**1953** Paul Kirk publishes *Crime Investigation*, one of the first comprehensive criminalistics and crime investigation texts.

**1967** The FBI National Crime Information Center (NCIC) becomes operational.

**1971** The photo-fit process, enabling eyewitnesses to piece together facial features as a means of identification, is developed by photographer Jacques Perry.

**1977** Masato Soba, in Japan, invents "super glue" fuming method of developing latent fingerprints.

**1978** Electro-static Detection Apparatus (ESDA) is used to expose invisible handwriting impressions on paper or any other surface, developed by Bob Freeman and Doug Foster.

**1986** In the first use of DNA to solve a murder, Dr. Alec Jeffreys uses DNA profiling to identify the killer of two young girls in the English Midlands.

**1987** Rapist Tommy Lee Andrews becomes the first American convicted through use of DNA profiling.

**1991** The Integrated Ballistics Identification System (IBIS), an automated imaging system for the comparison of the marks left on fired bullets, cartridge cases, and shell casings, is launched.

**1999** The FBI introduces the Integrated Automated Fingerprint Identification System (IAFIS), which allows storage and search capabilities via the national database.

   The Video Spectral Comparator is introduced, providing enhanced computerized means of examining questioned documents.

**2000** Low Copy Number analysis, developed in England, allows scientists to obtain a DNA profile from much smaller samples than was previously possible.

# Endnotes

## Introduction

1. Michael Baden and Marion Roach, *Dead Reckoning: The New Science of Catching Killers* (New York: Simon & Schuster, 2001).
2. Department of Justice, Federal Bureau of Investigation, "Crime Clock 2004," Federal Bureau of Investigation, http://www.fbi.gov/ucr/cius_04/summary/crime_clock/index.html (Accessed August 5, 2008).

## Chapter 3

1. *State of New York v. Angelo John LaMarca*, 3 N.Y.2d 452; 144 N.E.2d 420; 165 N.Y.S.2d 753; (1957 N.Y).
2. Ibid.
3. Anthony Scaduto, *Scapegoat* (New York: Putnam, 1976).
4. G.M. Laporte, "The Use of an Electrostatic Detection Device," *Journal of Forensic Sciences* 49, 3 (May 2004).

## Chapter 4

1. Alexander Feinberg, "Edison Clerk Finds Case In File," *New York Times*, January 23, 1957, p. 18.
2. Michael Horsnell, Stewart Tendler, and Frances Gibb, "Judge Attacks Police Over 'Murder Trap,'" *The Times* (London), September 15, 1994, p. 18.

## Chapter 5

1. W.A. Baillie-Grohman, "Ancient Weapons of the Chase," *The Burlington Magazine for Connoisseurs* 4, 12 (March 1904): 281.
2. U.S. Census Bureau, *The Statistical Abstract of the U.S. 2007*, U.S. Census Bureau, http://www.census.gov/compendia/statab/ (Accessed August 7, 2008).
3. Bob Hunter, "Judge Could Reverse Jury Verdict," *Chicago Daily Defender*, June 1, 1968, p. 28.
4. Bureau of Alcohol, Tobacco, Firearms, and Explosives, "ATF's NIBIN Program," National Integrated Ballistic Information Network, http://www.nibin.gov/nibin.pdf (Accessed April 28, 2008).

## Chapter 6

1. *State v. Zeigler*, 402 So. 2d 365; (1981 Fla).

## Chapter 7

1. "Star Witness Testifies in Tobacco Heir's Trial," *New York Times*, July 19, 1986, p. 8.

**Chapter 8**

1. Innocence Project, "Innocence Project Case Profiles," The Innocence Project, http://www.innocenceproject. org/know (Accessed August 5, 2008).

**Chapter 9**

1. Fernada Santos, "Evidence From Bite Marks, It Turns Out, Is Not So Elementary," *New York Times*, January 28, 2007, p. 41.

# Bibliography

Baden, Michael, and Judith Adler Hennessee. *Unnatural Death: Confessions of a Forensic Pathologist.* New York: Ballantine, 1989.

Cuthbert, C. R. M. *Science and the Detection of Crime.* London, U.K.: Hutchinson, 1958.

Di Maio, Vincent J. M. *Gunshot Wounds: Practical Aspects of Firearms, Ballistics, and Forensic Techniques.* New York: Elsevier Science Publishing Co., 1985.

Dower, Alan. *Crime Scientist.* London, U.K.: John Long, 1965.

Evans, Colin. *Blood on the Table: The Greatest Cases of New York City's Office of the Chief Medical Examiner.* New York: Berkley, 2008.

Evans, Colin. *The Casebook of Forensic Detection.* New York: Berkley, 2007.

Gaute, J. H. H., and Robin Odell. *Murder 'Whatdunit'.* London, U.K.: Harrap, 1982.

Gerber, Samuel, ed. *Chemistry and Crime: From Sherlock Holmes to Today's Courtroom.* Washington, D.C.: American Chemical Society, 1983.

Innes, Brian. *Bodies of Evidence.* Leicester, U.K.: Silverdale, 2000.

Jackson, Robert. *Francis Camps: Famous Case Histories of the Celebrated Pathologist.* London, U.K.: Hart-Davis MacGibbon, 1975.

Lane, Brian. *Encyclopedia of Forensic Science.* London, U.K.: Headline, 1992.

Lee, Henry C., Timothy Palmbach, and Marilyn T. Miller. *Henry Lee's Crime Scene Handbook.* London, U.K.: Academic, 2001.

Marriner, Brian. *Forensic Clues to Murder.* London, U.K.: Arrow, 1991.

Morland, Nigel. *Science in Crime Detection.* London, U.K.: Hale, 1958.

Saferstein, Richard. *Criminalistics: An Introduction to Forensic Science.* Upper Saddle River, N.J.: Prentice Hall, 1998.

Smith, Sir Sydney. *Mostly Murder.* London, U.K.: Harrap, 1959.

Smyth, Frank. *Cause of Death.* London, U.K.: Pan Books, 1982.

Thompson, John. *Crime Scientist.* London, U.K.: Harrap & Co., 1980.

Thorwald, Jürgen. *The Century of the Detective.* New York: Harcourt, Brace & World, 1965.

Wecht, Cyril, Mark Curriden, and Benjamin Wecht. *Cause of Death.* New York: Dutton, 1993.

Wilson, Colin. *Written in Blood: A History of Forensic Detection.* New York: Carroll & Graf, 2003.

# Further Resources

## Books

Bass, William M., and Jon Jefferson. *Death's Acre: Inside the Legendary 'Body Farm.'* New York: Putnam, 2003.

Beavan, Colin. *Fingerprints: The Origins of Crime Detection and the Murder Case that Launched Forensic Science.* New York: Hyperion, 2001.

Bowers, C. Michael, and Gary Bell. *Manual of Forensic Odontology.* Saratoga Springs, N.Y.: American Society of Forensic Odontology, 1997.

Brussel, James A. *Casebook of a Crime Psychiatrist.* New York: Grove Press, 1968.

Butler, John M. *Forensic DNA Typing.* Boston: Elsevier Academic Press, 2005.

Evans, Colin. *Killer Doctors.* New York: Berkley, 2007.

Glaister, John, and James Brash. *Medico-Legal Aspects of the Ruxton Case.* Edinburgh, U.K.: Livingstone, 1937.

Hilton, Ordway. *Scientific Examination of Questioned Documents.* New York: Elsevier, 1982.

Keppel, Robert D. *Offender Profiling.* Mason, Ohio: Thomson, 2006.

Lewis, Alfred Allan, and Herbert MacDonell. *The Evidence Never Lies.* New York: Holt, Rinehart and Winston, 1984.

Nafte, Myriam. *Flesh and Bone: An Introduction to Forensic Anthropology.* Durham: Carolina Academic Press, 2000.

Ratha, Nalini, and Rudd Bolle. *Automatic Fingerprint Recognition System.* New York: Springer, 2004.

Ressler, Robert K., and Thomas Schachtman. *Whoever Fights Monsters.* New York: St. Martin's Press, 1992.

Rinker, Robert A. *Understanding Firearm Ballistics.* Croydon, Ind.: Mulberry House, 2005.

Schiller, Bill. *A Hand in the Water: The Many Lies of Albert Walker.* New York: HarperCollins, 1999.

Simpson, Keith. *Forty Years of Murder.* New York: Scribner, 1979.

Wambaugh, Joseph. *The Blooding.* New York: Morrow, 1989.

Watson, James D., and Andrew Berry. *DNA: The Secret of Life.* New York: Knopf, 2003.

Wonder, Anita. *Bloodstain Pattern Evidence.* San Diego: Academic Press, 2007.

Yinon, Jehuda. *Forensic and Environmental Detection of Explosives.* New York: Wiley, 1999.

## Court Cases

*State v. Zeigler,* 494 So. 2d 957, (1986 Fla.).

*People v. Branion, Appellant,* 47 Ill. 2d 70; 265 N.E.2d 1; (1970 Ill).

*People v. Jennings,* 252 Ill. 534, 96 N.E. 1077, (1911 Ill.).

## Web Sites

Bureau of Alcohol, Firearms, Tobacco and Explosives. "Arson & Explosives."
http://www.atf.treas.gov/explarson/index.htm

Dorman, Michael. "Held for Ransom," *Newsday* Online.
http://www.newsday.com/community/guide/lihistory/ny-history-hsfwein,0,2329983.story.

Federal Bureau of Investigation. "Famous Cases."
http://www.fbi.gov/libref/historic/famcases/weinber/weinbernew.htm.

Tony Café Forensic. "Aids Used for Detecting Accelerants at Fire Scenes."
http://www.tcforensic.com.au/docs/article4.html.

# Index

Foster, Edward  22
Freeman, Bob  106
*Frye v. United States*  29
fuse  82

**G**

Galton, Francis  28–29, 104
gas chromatography (GC)  81, 106
Geco ammunition  59, 60
gel electrophoresis  91
gender, indicators from skeletal remains  37
genetic markers  88
Gill, Augustus  61
Glaister, John  31, 36
Gleason, Albert  77, 79
Gleser, Goldine  38
global positioning system (GPS)  96–97
Goddard, Calvin  61, 105
Goddard, Henry  104
Graflex Speed Graphic  15
Gravelle, Phillip O.  61, 65, 105
grooves  59, 62, 65
Gross, Hans  68, 70, 104
gunpowder  62, 81
gunshot wounds  63, 73

**H**

Hall, Albert Llewellyn  62
Hamilton, Dawn  90
handwriting analysis  42–46
Hauptmann, Bruno Richard  44–46
height, of corpse  38
helixometer  61
Henry, Edward  29, 105
Herophilus  103
Herschel, William  27, 104
high explosives  82
high velocity spatter  72
Hill, Timothy  99
Hiller, Clarence  19, 21–22
Hiller, Clarice  19
Hiller, Florence  19
Hi Standard  59
Hitler, Adolf  54–55
Holland, Mary  22
Hooks, William, III  60

*Hsi Duan Yu* (the Washing Away of Wrongs)  103
hypostasis (livor mortis)  97, 100

**I**

identification  30–39
Illinois Supreme Court  22
impact angle  73–74
infanticide  103
ink  47
Innocence Project  90
Integrated Automated Fingerprint Identification System (IAFIS)  27
Integrated Ballistics Identification System (IBIS)  65, 106
International Association for Criminal Identification  105
International Association of Chiefs of Police (IACP)  104–105
International Ink Library  47

**J**

Jackson, Harry  105
James, A. T.  106
Jeffreys, Alec  87–89, 106
Jennings, Thomas  20–22
jet fuel  84
Johnson, Henry (alias)  18

**K**

Keeler, Leonard  105
Kelly, Alice G.  50, 52
Kelly, Ian  88, 89
Kelly, Joyce  60
Kendall, Carol Lynn  76, 79
Kentra, Theresa  59
Kerston, Alvin  59
kidnapping  40–48
Kirchoff, Gustav  104
Kirk, Paul Leland  106
knife  73
Kretschmer, Ernst  54
Kürten, Peter  54

**L**

Laboratory Information Management System (LIMS)  20
*The Lady Jane* (boat)  96, 97
LaMarca, Angelo John  43–44, 46

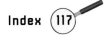

# About the Author

Colin Evans is the author of numerous articles and books that deal with the history and development of forensic science. He has written *Blood on the Table: The Greatest Cases of New York City's Office of the Chief Medical Examiner*, *The Casebook of Forensic Detection*, and *The Father of Forensics: The Groundbreaking Cases of Sir Bernard Spilsbury and the Beginnings of Modern CSI*, and others. He lives in the United Kingdom.

To find out more, visit his Web site at http://www.colin-evans online.com

# About the Consulting Editor

John L. French is a 31-year veteran of the Baltimore City Police Crime Laboratory. He is currently a crime laboratory supervisor. His responsibilities include responding to crime scenes, overseeing the preservation and collection of evidence and training crime scene technicians. He has been actively involved in writing the operating procedures and technical manual for his unit and has conducted training in numerous areas of crime scene investigation. In addition to his crime scene work, Mr. French is also a published author, specializing in crime fiction. His short stories have appeared in *Alfred Hitchcock's Mystery Magazine* and numerous anthologies.